AF437136

THE NOTORIOUS Adams Boys

The True Story of Country Music's Original Band of Brothers

A Memoir By:

ERIC GRATE

Foreword by Ralph May

The Notorious Adams Boys

First Edition: April, 2026

Published by Coal Shed Publishing, Danville, KY USA

ISBN: 979-8-9883716-5-6 (Paperback)

ISBN: 979-8-9883716-4-9 (Hardcover)

Library of Congress Control Number: 2026911375

Book Cover design by Michelle Grate

Editor: Michelle Grate

Cover Photo: Arnie Adams, Gary Adams, Don Adams, circa 1964, courtesy of Don Adams

www.ericgrate.com

Printed in the USA

PART THREE
Between the Legends

Contents

Circa: 1965 Courtesy of Doug Jernigan
Top: Doug Jernigan
Middle: Arnie Adams, Gary Adams
Bottom: Don Adams

Dedication

This book is dedicated to the memory of the Adams Boys:
Roland Edward "Arnie" Adams 1937–2023
Donald Eugene Adams 1941–2026
Gary Harlan Adams 1943–2022

Quotes

"Gary was an amazing player who always projected this sense of super coolness. Had a real dry sense of humor. Even though he played in country bands, he loved to show off his jazz prowess. Once in a while, we'd play together in this rundown after-hours club in Nashville called Gabe's. We'd see who could play the fastest. He'd say, "C'mon, boy, let's go lock horns!". I pity the singer who tried to sing through all that, haha."
Brent Mason
Guitarist and Songwriter
November 8, 2025

Quotes

"When I was 23 yrs old, and I'd started in that band, I got a 10 or 20-year shortcut that other guys didn't have, between Don and Gary. I mean the things they had picked up and learned (...) I just picked that up at once. I didn't have to spend 20 years learning that like they did. They were mentors.

And I've always been grateful. (...) It just made me such a more proficient singer and player. By just watching them, observing them and seeing how they done things. I got a crash course there, buddy. I'm still thankful for that. "

Mike "Cutty" Cutright
Longtime Adams Boys Associate
July 21, 2025

Foreword

By: Ralph May

The Adams boys: Gary, Don, and Arnie, came from the wrong side of the tracks in Greenfield, Ohio. They left town and played some of the biggest stages in America. Carnegie Hall. Madison Square Garden. The Grand Ole Opry. They put their stamp on country music, and then came back to Greenfield.

I knew the Adams boys for over sixty years, as friends and as fellow musicians. Like countless other boys from Greenfield, I was inspired by their success and Johnny Paycheck's, enough to pursue my own career in music.

I remember George Jones' tour bus rolling into town, and Don Adams' Cadillac pulling a white trailer behind it, "George Jones and the Jones Boys, Featuring Don Adams" stenciled on the back. I remember sitting outside Paul Angel's house, listening to music drift up from his basement. I remember thinking, that could be me someday.

Later, I was fortunate to share the stage with Gary and Don, opening for Johnny Paycheck and playing in bands we put together over the years. I saw firsthand what made them great: the discipline, the talent, the hunger to play no matter who was listening or where the gig was.

The Adams Boys backed George Jones, Johnny Paycheck, Ray Price, Little Jimmy Dickens, Marty Robbins, and so many others during country music's golden era. Their story is wild, funny, heartbreaking, and worth telling.

Eric Grate was born and raised in Greenfield. He grew up listening to the music and hearing the stories. As a writer, he knows how to take these stories and create something that pulls you in and won't let go. He interviewed more than twenty-five people for this book, musicians, family members, eyewitnesses, and wove their perspectives into a narrative that isn't just facts and dates. It's alive. It's the Adams Boys as they were: talented and notorious.

The Notorious Adams Boys is a great read for country music fans, for anyone who loves a good story.

I hope you enjoy it as much as I do.

Ralph May

April 4, 2026

** Ralph May is well known in country music, having performed in the mid-1970s alongside the Adams Boys and the legendary Johnny Paycheck, and on his own with country music superstar Tammy Wynette. Ralph has recorded with major music labels including Ovation, AMI, and Oak Records while landing on the Billboard Country Music Top 100 chart five times between 1981 and 1987 with the songs "Cajun Lady," "In a Stranger's Eyes," "Here Comes That Feeling Again," "Angels Get Lonely Too," and "Memory Attack." In 1985, Ralph moved to California, where he formed the Ohio River Band, signed with Five Star Productions, and opened for prominent recording artists across Southern California. In 2024, Ralph was inducted into the Ohio Country Music Hall of Fame. Now retired, Ralph and his lovely wife, Tina, reside in Washington Court House, OH.*

Preface

My wife, Michelle, and I were driving to Lexington when I got a message from Don Adams. The message said, "Eric, call me at this number." So, I called the number.

When Don answered the phone, he said, "Eric, we need to write a book."

Our First Interview Eric Grate and Don Adams Greenfield, OH February 22, 2025 Photo by Eric Grate

I said, "Don, what do we need to write a book about?"

He said, "The Notorious Adams Boys, and I want to tell it all!"

I explained to Don that I'm a fiction writer and I've never written a non-fiction book before. I asked him why he thought I should write the book.

He said, "Because you're from Greenfield, you'll understand."

I told Don I needed a day to think about it, but I had already decided in my mind that I was going to write the book.

Acknowledgements

Thank you to Don Adams. Brother, getting to know you over the 50 weeks that we spent together as friends will stand forever as one of the highlights of my life. You were a perfect example of a man displaying strength and perseverance during personal trials. I'll never forget you.

Thank you to my wife, Michelle. You sacrificed your time and energy and supported me faithfully during the 15 months we spent writing this book. If not for you, I couldn't have done it and probably wouldn't have tried.

At the risk of leaving out some deserving person, I want to thank those who contributed to the book through their stories and insights. I'm talking about the family members, friends, fans, and fellow musicians who shared their lives with the Adams Boys.

Brent Adams, Missi Adams, Brad Adams, Dee Shelton, Kim Adams, Kandi Adams, Stephanie Adams Roggero, Gary Adams Jr. (Little Gary), Farrell Adams, Darrell Adams, Steve Marple, Faye Marple (That's Faye. F.A.Y.E. Faye.), Randy Adams, Judy McCarty, Doug Jernigan, Ralph May, Mike Cutright, Diane McCall, Dee Jee Overby, Brent Mason, Herb Day, Jackie Thomas, Kevin Smith, Randy Angel, Jim Bristley, Greg Smith, and Lloyd Bowers

Introduction

Texas must have a thousand or more honky-tonks and dance halls scattered among small towns and big cities alike. Dallas, Tyler, Houston, Galveston, Bandera, New Braunfels, San Antonio... Last night it was Corpus Christi. Tonight, it's Abilene. Tomorrow night it's Austin. One after the other. The twenty-seventh in a string of thirty-one shows in thirty-eight days. Twenty-eight hundred miles separate the first show from the last. Like the spokes in a spinning wheel, each one is different, but each one is the same.

Four hundred people fill the dance hall to capacity. Most sit at tables around the large dance floor, talking, laughing, drinking beer, and waiting for the music to start again. Others gather near the stage for a good view and holler requests at the band.

The crowd represents a cross-section of Texas society: hard-looking men just off their shifts in the oil fields, cowboys (and I mean the real kind) ready to unwind after a long day, men in suits and shiny boots fresh from their corporate offices downtown, and football players from Abilene Christian University who are violating curfew. Among them are enough Texas beauties to prove once and for all that God truly did bless Texas.

Don Adams stands on stage, surveying the crowd. The voices, laughter, and the sounds of shuffling feet blend into the smoky haze hanging in the air.

The band performing on stage with Don, who sings and plays bass guitar, is widely regarded as the top touring country-western band in America. Don's younger brother, Gary Adams, is just 21 and already considered one of the best guitarists in country music. He exudes confidence and a cocky demeanor on stage; always grinning. Their older brother, Roland Adams, known as Arnie or "Big Arnie," has perfect timing and plays the drums. Buddy Emmons, who is destined to become the greatest steel guitarist of all time, is also on stage. The talented fiddle player is Charlie Justice.

To Don, it feels like he and his brothers are a world away from Greenfield, Ohio, the tough, working-class town they grew up in. A place where the number of beer joints is rivaled only by the number of churches, making it convenient to those seeking forgiveness on Sunday morning for the sins they committed on Saturday night.

Don gazes out into the dance hall. Muffled sounds: the chatter, the laughs, the scooting of chairs across the worn wood floor. Distant memories in sepia tones cycle through Don's mind at three-quarters speed, like snapshots in time. He thinks of his father, Frank Adams, an accomplished fiddle player who chose to work in a factory rather than pursue a life of music on the road, all to support his wife and their nine children. He recalls his mother, Kate, who raised all nine kids while instilling in them a deep sense of faith in God. He remembers his brothers and sisters, often crowded two or three to a bed, sharing the one guitar that their father had bought for them. A particular memory stands out when he thinks of Gary hiding the family's one guitar, making sure none of the others would play it while he was distracted.

Don closes his eyes and hears the sounds of his father's fiddle drifting into his bedroom. Frank got up every morning and played his fiddle before going to work. It drove 12-year-old Don crazy, and he often asked his mother to

"PLEASE ask Daddy not to play his fiddle in the morning." Standing on that stage, Don cherishes the memory and the melancholy feeling it imparts.

The reality before him sets in and Don says, "We're going to do one more before we bring George back out. This is a Buck Owens song called 'Act Naturally!'" As the band begins to play, couples rush to the dance floor. Don sings, *"They're gonna put me in the movies..."*

In 1964, George Jones was America's top-selling country singer, a title he held for three consecutive years. His band, the Jones Boys, supported him throughout this journey, performing hundreds of shows each year at venues across the country. From sunny Florida to frigid Minnesota, from Midwestern fairgrounds to Madison Square Garden, and from East Coast nightclubs to honky-tonks and dance halls throughout the American Southwest, enthusiastic crowds would flock to see "GEORGE JONES AND THE JONES BOYS FEATURING DON ADAMS" wherever it appeared on the marquee.

The three Adams brothers, 23-year-old Don, 21-year-old Gary, and 25-year-old Arnie, grew up in a musical family. It seems natural for them to be touring the country alongside the biggest country music star in the world. However, if you take a closer look, you'll see that in just over two years, they went from performing in dive bars and family restaurants to appearing on television and playing at prestigious venues like the Hollywood Bowl and Madison Square Garden. How did this happen for three boys who grew up so close to the wrong side of the tracks?

It isn't an easy life for Don and Arnie as they both have wives and kids to worry about, and bills to pay back home. Gary, though, is a young single guy with no ties, bound only to playing music and having fun. Home to him is whatever hotel room he's sleeping in at the time. Although the lines occasionally get blurred, those ties and lack of ties will go on to shape the individual musical careers of all three brothers over the next 25 years or more.

With the show over and the crowd gone, Don, Gary, Arnie, and their bandmates do what they do after every show. They pack away their gear, get in their car, and drive a hundred miles or more to another town where they will do it all again. The twenty-eighth in a string of thirty-one shows in thirty-eight days. Then it's back home to whatever awaits them in Greenfield. But only for a few days. The West Coast is calling, and so is Canada, and New York, and New England.

The Adams brothers have a good friend in the country music world: Donald Eugene Lytle, who is also from Greenfield. His family's home was a literal stone's throw from the Adams family home. Lytle's stage name is Donny Young. Later, he will call himself Johnny Paycheck and become famous and infamous at the same time. The Adams Boys will play a major role in his career, sharing both the good times and the bad. Keep in mind that Donald (Donnie) Lytle, Donny Young, and Johnny Paycheck are the same person at different stages of life throughout the book

Besides George Jones and Johnny Paycheck, the Adams Boys will go on to tour the country with the likes of Merle Haggard, Little Jimmy Dickens, Ferlin Husky, Marty Robbins, and others. Along the way, they will weave a story that will become a legend, complete with all the trappings and tinged with myth.

There will be good times and bad times: Don will knock George Jones out cold in a Texas parking lot and place five songs on the Billboard Country Chart. Gary will confront Michael Landon on stage and write hit songs with Johnny Paycheck. Arnie will lock Little Jimmy Dickens in a closet and play with him at Carnegie Hall.

The songs, the fights, the firings, the successes, the failures, the truth, and the lies. It all comes together to form an incredible tale that Don could not even imagine while standing on that Texas stage in 1964.

PART ONE

The Early Years

Coal Shed Publishing

Chapter 1

Getting Started

F rank and Kate Adams had ten children, all born within a few miles of Greenfield, OH. Their oldest child, Howard, was born in 1935, followed by Sharon in 1936, Roland*** (better known as Arnie) in 1937, Eldon (known as Wayne) in 1939, Donald (commonly referred to as Don) in 1941, Marciline (nicknamed Marcie) in 1942, Gary in 1943, Hester (known as Elaine) in 1945, and Farrell and Darrell, (twins) in 1947. Tragically, Sharon passed away at just six weeks old, leaving Frank and Kate with nine children to raise.

1

The Adams Siblings (L to R) Farrell, Darrell, Elaine, Gary, Marcie, Don, Wayne, Arnie, Howard. Circa 1971 Courtesy of Lisa Haney and Gary Adams Jr.

---

1. ***Note: Roland was better known as "Arnie." He acquired the name from two friends, Randy Angel and Tommy Rambo, who bestowed it on him in 1961. The three friends were watching the movie *King of the Roaring '20s, The Story of Arnold Rothstein* at The Ranch Drive-In in Greenfield, OH. Randy and Tommy thought that Roland (Arnie) bore a striking resemblance to David Janssen, the actor playing Arnold Rothstein. So, they started calling him "Big Arnie," and it stuck. Arnie's oldest son, Brad Adams, who was 6 at the time, was also there and remembers it quite well. For simplicity's sake, I will refer to Roland as Arnie throughout the book.

The family moved frequently, averaging about every two years. Don recalled instances when Frank would leave for work in the morning, and by the time he returned home that evening, Kate had already relocated the family. Don remembered most of the homes they lived in, but he often struggled to recall the exact time they lived there unless a memorable event was associated with a particular house.

Don said that his earliest memory is of waking up before sunrise to the sound of his father, Frank, playing the fiddle before heading off to work. "He got up every morning at five o'clock and played his fiddle. After getting ready for work, he would sit in the kitchen and play for an hour." I asked Don if this was a good memory for him.

"It's a good memory, but I hated it at the time. I was trying to sleep, and there he would go with that fiddle. I begged Mommy to make him stop, but he never did," he said.

I found it touching when Don, at 84, called his parents "Daddy" and "Mommy."

When Don was about six years old, he sat down with his family one evening to eat supper. "I remember being excited because there was meat on the table," Don recalled. "We were poor, and we didn't get meat very often, so when we did, we appreciated it."

As the family enjoyed their meal, young Don said, "This is some really good chicken."

The comment made his older brothers chuckle. When Don asked what was so funny, one of them replied, "That's not chicken; it's rabbit."

"Mom had cooked our pet rabbits, Clyde and Virgil. I didn't eat another bite, and it was years before I ate rabbit again. It took me a while to get over that. But Mommy figured we had to eat," said Don.

At about the same time, Frank purchased the family's first guitar. All the children began learning to play, but Don and Gary were more enthusiastic about it than the others.

"Daddy taught us how to play," said Don. "He'd play the fiddle, and we'd play rhythm guitar. Any time we fell behind or hit a bad note, he would reach out with his bow and whack us on the head with it to get our attention."

Frank and his brother, John Adams, played music together. They often sang at local churches alongside Kate and sometimes opened for country stars performing in the area. One memorable show took place on August 28, 1948, at the Lyric Theater in Greenfield, where they opened for Tex Ritter and his horse, White Flash.

Frank and John also hosted a radio show on WCHO Radio in Washington Court House, Ohio. The show aired every Saturday morning at 10:30 AM. It was during this show, around 1949, that Don and Gary performed on the radio for the first time. Don was eight, and Gary was six. They sang a song titled "Pig Latin Serenade," a silly song recorded by the duo Johnny and Jack. The lyrics are a mix of English and Pig Latin and are rather suggestive. For example: "*We'll go down to the Lovers Lane, and we'll make love, and Pa won't know, and Ma won't care.*"

Along with their Saturday morning radio show, the two boys, their dad, and uncle also performed on Saturday nights at the jamboree in Washington Court House.

The Adams family faced severe poverty during the childhoods of the Adams boys, and this topic often arose in conversations between Don and me, particularly when reflecting on their early years.

To illustrate just how poor the family was during that time, one need only consider this: In 1950, when Don was nine years old, Kate served groundhog for Christmas dinner. "Not a single bite was taken," Don recalled. "Not even Mom ate it."

Despite the family's financial struggles, they occasionally acquired luxuries. One such example was a horse that Frank purchased around 1951 as a family pet.

"Daddy bought a horse off some guy, complete with saddle and all," Don said. "We were living outside of Frankfort (about 15 miles east of Greenfield) at the time, and a couple of days after Daddy brought the horse home, Mommy decided it was time to move again. So we moved to a house near Good Hope (about 10 miles north of Greenfield)."

The family faced one problem during their move to Good Hope: they didn't own a horse trailer, which meant they had no way to transport their horse the 17 miles to their new home. The only reasonable solution was for someone to ride the horse to Good Hope.

"My brother, Howard, saddled the horse up and rode it from Frankfort to Good Hope," Don said.

"Did Howard know how to ride a horse?" I asked.

"Nope. He had never ridden one before."

"Did he make it okay?"

"Yeah, he made it," Don answered. "He was probably a little sore when he got there."

The boys first appeared on stage in 1952 at a minstrel show at Good Hope School. Don was 11, and Gary was 9.

A minstrel show is a performance where white entertainers wear blackface. While it's difficult to imagine today, this was common in the early 1950s.

Gary refused to paint his face black because he was afraid the paint wouldn't come off. Don didn't paint his face either because he didn't want to look different than Gary. They were the only two performers on the show who weren't in blackface. Once again, they sang "Pig Latin Serenade."

In 1954, the Adams family moved again, this time to a farmhouse located between Greenfield and Leesburg in Highland County. Don began the ninth grade at Fairfield High School in Leesburg, but soon contracted pneumonia. Unfortunately, he missed the entire school year as a result.

Don and Gary took the stage again on March 29, 1955, during the Jaycees Talent Contest at the McClain High School Auditorium. However, an article in the *Greenfield Daily Times* on March 30, 1955, mistakenly referred to Gary as Jerry Adams. They were advertised as a "vocalist and guitarist."

According to the *Greenfield Daily Times* from March 31, 1955, the winners of the local talent competition were a vocal girls' trio from Marshall, who took home a $50 cash prize. Second place was awarded to Harold Barnhart and Bobby Walker, a guitar-and-mandolin duo from Greenfield, who received $25. Third place went to pantomimist Virginia Groves, who was awarded $15. Don and Gary finished out of the money.

The talent show remains a common topic of conversation in Greenfield today, with various versions of the story circulating. Most claim that Johnny Paycheck, then known as Donald Lytle, performed alongside Don and Gary, not as a vocalist but as a guitarist. However, none of the articles I referenced mentions him.

Additionally, most stories have the Adams-Lytle trio finishing second to a female tap dancer. Once again, I couldn't find any reference to a female tap dancer.

It's possible that there was another talent contest featuring young Lytle, where he experienced a heartbreaking defeat to a girl tap dancer. However, I couldn't find any record of this event.

Around the same time as the talent show, Don began visiting Club 28, Paul Angel's bar located on West Jefferson Street at the edge of Greenfield, every Friday night. He would bum a quarter from his dad for this outing. Although Don was only 14 or 15 years old, Paul allowed him to come in and use the quarter in the jukebox. With a quarter, Don could play six songs, and he always chose Wynn Stewart's "Keeper of the Keys," playing it six times in a row. After the last play of the song, Paul would ask Don to leave.

Around this time, the Adams family moved into a neighborhood on the west end of South Street known as the Mayfair Addition. Their house was located next to the B&O Railroad tracks, directly across from an unincorporated area called Higginsville. Living in a house on Foraker Street in Higginsville, just a stone's throw away, was a young man named Donald Eugene Lytle, who would later become known worldwide as Johnny Paycheck.

During this period, Don would gather with Gary, Donnie Lytle, Joe Adams (the Adams boys' cousin), and a few other boys from the area to play music together.

Don described growing up with Donnie Lytle as, "Growing up on different sides of the tracks, with both sides being the wrong side."

Don started the ninth grade once again, this time at McClain High School in Greenfield. For the second consecutive year, he contracted pneumonia, which forced him to miss several weeks of school. After that, Don never returned to school. Instead, he took a job with a small company that washed bread pans for Pennington's Bakery in Washington Court House.

Don and Gary continued to share the family guitar, but Gary tried hard to keep it in his possession as much as possible.

"Gary wouldn't take his hands off that guitar," Don said. "He played it night and day. He played at least 15 hours a day. Sometimes he would hide it so no one else could find it. He would even take it to the outhouse with him."

Needless to say, Gary quickly became the family's best guitar player. Don reflected on that fact years later when he said to me, "I didn't want to play bass. But Gary was a damn good guitar player, and we didn't need two guitarists."

By 1957, Don and Gary, along with several other young musicians from the Greenfield area, including their sister, Marcie, were performing together at school dances and teen hangouts. They spent a significant amount of time practicing with Donnie Lytle (also known as Donny Young and Johnny Paycheck) at Paul Angel's house in Greenfield. It was there that Donnie introduced Don and Gary to a talented young singer and musician named Darrell McCall. McCall lived in New Jasper Township, Ohio, about 35 miles north of Greenfield in Greene County. Like Donnie and the Adams brothers, McCall performed throughout the area and secured a radio program on WCHO Radio in nearby Washington Court House.

Don and Gary quickly became good friends with McCall, and the McCall family home in New Jasper turned into a popular hangout for the four of them and other local musicians.

Mrs. McCall welcomed them and encouraged their music playing, but she frowned upon misbehavior and, under no circumstances, allowed alcohol in her home.

At the age of fourteen or fifteen, Gary met McCall's younger sister, Diane, who was a year younger than he was. They were mutually attracted to each other and quickly became a couple. As a result, Gary began spending a lot of time at the McCall residence. Diane's mother even allowed him to stay overnight, though he had to sleep on the living room floor, separate from Diane, who didn't really want Gary to stay overnight.

"I wanted him to woo me, not sleep on our floor," Diane said.

Since Gary didn't have a driver's license or a car, he relied on various means to travel from Greenfield to New Jasper. This included rides from his brother, Don, and his cousins Larry "Red Dog" Adams and Phil Hill, and hitchhiking whenever he had to.

On April 25, 2025, Michelle and I traveled to Nashville to interview Diane McCall and her sister, Dee Jee McCall Overby, for our book. Dee Jee shared a funny story about Gary and Red Dog during one of their trips to Jasper Mills.

The boys had acquired an old Buick automobile, which they had painted with primer and spray-painted the word "DEATH" in black on the hood. The word was written so that oncoming cars could easily read it.

They drove from Greenfield, and when they were just a couple of miles from Jasper Mills, Gary convinced Red Dog to get out of the car and stand by the side of the road. The idea was for Red Dog to watch as Gary sped past, first in one direction and then in the other. This was meant to help Red Dog appreciate how good the car looked while it was moving.

After a few passes, they planned for Gary to pull over and switch places with Red Dog so that Red Dog could drive the car while Gary watched it go by. However, on what was supposed to be his last pass before switching, Gary slowed down as if he were going to stop, then suddenly punched the accelerator and drove straight to Diane's house, leaving Red Dog standing on the side of the road.

When Gary arrived at Diane's house, he went inside and asked her to come out and see what he had brought for her. Diane, expecting something nice, was not thrilled by the "DEATH car," but she stayed outside on the porch to chat with Gary. About an hour later, a very angry barefoot Red Dog approached the porch while Gary retreated to the other side of the yard to mock and laugh at him. Without hesitation, Red Dog entered the house and retrieved a large kitchen knife. He used it to cut every wire, belt, and hose he could reach under the hood of the car.

In July 1959, Donnie Lytle and Darrell McCall traveled to Nashville, where they adopted the stage names Donny and Darrell Young and performed as a duo. The experience was rough, and after a short time, Donnie returned to Ohio.

While back in Greenfield, Donnie took a job at Collins Meatpacking Plant, where he worked alongside Arnie Adams, who was not yet involved in music.

After working for a week and receiving his first paycheck, Donnie decided to go with Arnie to Paul Angel's Club 28 to relax and have a few beers. Donnie was in a jovial mood, feeling proud of his hard work and the pay he earned.

As they chatted, Donnie said to Arnie, "You know, this isn't bad. This is how a man is supposed to live, ain't it?"

"Well," Arnie replied. "It's the only way I know how to live."

One week later, after receiving his second paycheck, Donnie left town and returned to Nashville. So much for how a man is supposed to live.

In the fall of 1959, Don, Gary, Marcie, their friend Gary Kniesly, and a couple of other guys from Greenfield performed at a dance in Blanchester, Ohio, 32 miles west of Greenfield along State Route 28.

Towards the end of the evening, while the band was on break, a local boy approached the edge of the stage and began plucking the strings of Gary Adams' guitar. Don asked the boy to stop, but he continued. In response, Don pushed the boy, knocking him to the ground.

After finishing their show, the band loaded all their equipment into Don's 1952 Dodge and began their journey back to Greenfield from Blanchester. A line of five or six cars followed them out of town, and somewhere between Blanchester and New Vienna, two of the cars overtook Don and blocked the road ahead.

"A couple of them passed us," Don said, "So, I just ran into one of their cars. All these guys piled out of their cars and me and Gary Kniesly, and the other guys jumped out of my car to fight them. One of them had a chain and was swinging it around. A few of them jumped on me, and one of them hit me so hard it broke my nose and tore the seat out of my pants when I hit the asphalt. They kicked my ribs and roughed me up pretty bad. One of them even hit Marcie"

Don laughed as he shared this story.

"Brother," I said, "we need to make sure this scene makes it into the movie they're gonna make out of this book."

"Well," Don continued, "Gary (Adams) slid over into the driver's seat, and he was trying to run over these guys. He had the car down in the ditch chasing them. He would have run over them and not thought twice about it."

"That was a pretty bad beatdown," I said.

Don laughed again and said, "The worst part was my broken nose. They laid my nose clear over flat on the side of my face. I still suffer from that and have to wear nasal strips to breathe when I sleep."

Around the same time as the Blanchester beatdown, Don and Gary began performing in the area alongside Paul Angel and a few other local musicians. They primarily played at dances and bars in Greenfield, Hillsboro, Chillicothe, Wilmington, and other nearby towns.

Then, in 1960, they got together with a country singer from nearby Bowersville, OH, named Paul Wayne, whose real name was Paul Borst. Wayne was signed to Starday Records and was playing shows in Dayton and Columbus, as well as making sporadic trips to Nashville to record.

Wayne's band consisted of Gary on lead guitar, Don on bass and harmony vocals, and Joe Adams on steel guitar. Don said he couldn't remember who was playing drums at first, but he knew the guy who would soon take over at drums quite well.

One evening, shortly after joining Paul Wayne, Don, Gary, and Joe were rehearsing at Wayne's house. Arnie came along for the ride, and midway through their rehearsal, Wayne noticed Arnie tapping his foot on the floor and his finger on a table, keeping time with the music. After the rehearsal ended, Wayne approached Arnie and mentioned that he thought Arnie would make a good drummer. He suggested that Arnie join them for their next rehearsal and give it a try. Although Arnie wasn't playing music yet, he spoke to Don, Gary, and Joe about it on the way home, and they encouraged him to go for it.

The very next day, Arnie bought a used snare drum in Greenfield and began practicing by playing along with records. He then began joining his brothres at Paul Angel's house for their regular jam sessions. From there, he went to rehearsals at Paul Wayne's house, and just like that, Arnie Adams became a drummer.

Arnie Adams on a tour bus. Circa 1964
Courtesy of Brent and Missi Adams

In late summer of 1961, Paul Wayne and the Adams Boys Band, composed of Don, Gary, Arnie, and Joe, traveled to Decatur, Illinois, for a two-week engagement at a local nightclub. This marked the first time the Adams Boys performed on the road.

The man who booked the engagement told him that there wouldn't "be much more than bean money" for pay, but that it would be a good experience and would almost certainly lead to bigger and better opportunities.

According to Don, those two weeks in Decatur were, in fact, a good experience, but they did not get paid. Not even bean money.

"The guy who booked it disappeared on the last night and took the money with him. We didn't make a dime."

"Paul Wayne was never able to get the money back?" I asked.

"Nope," Don answered. "Paul never saw the guy again."

By early 1961, the boys were still performing sporadic shows with Wayne, and Don provided harmony vocals on several of Wayne's records. Primarily, though, they played in nightclubs in Dayton and Columbus on their own, promoting themselves under various names, including The Adams Brothers, the Adams Boys Band, or Don Adams and the Adams Band.

The Adams Boys were making a name for themselves across southern and central Ohio, and soon fans in other parts of the country would find out just how good they were.

Chapter 2

Starstruck

After being fired by Ray Price, Donny Young, who was then signed to Mercury Records, made another attempt to launch his solo career. After a few months of inactivity, his booking agent, Bobby Boyd, secured him a six-week engagement in Las Vegas. He was set to perform six nights a week at the Nashville Nevada Club, a casino partly owned by country music star Wynn Stewart. The engagement was scheduled from November 11 to December 23. Donny reached out to his old friends, the Adams brothers, and invited them to join him as his band.

Donny originally planned for the group to barnstorm across the country, picking up gigs along the way. However, something changed his mind, and now they were driving straight to Las Vegas. The three Adams brothers, along with their cousin Larry Adams, nicknamed Red Dog, set out from Greenfield in Arnie's car during the week of November 4.

Their first stop was Nashville to pick up Donny, then they continued to Las Vegas.

Donny's decision to abandon his plan to barnstorm across America left the group in significant financial trouble, as none of them had much money to begin with. However, Donny did have a backup plan: he had brought along a stack of checks that he had stolen from his publisher, Tree Publishing, to fund the trip.

The group set out for Las Vegas with Donny writing checks as needed for gas, food, and lodging along the way. The trip took two days, with everyone taking turns driving. Upon arrival, they learned that Wynn Stewart would play the evening show each night, and that they would perform from midnight to 3:00 AM. I asked Don how many people attended the club at that hour. He replied that "Las Vegas was a twenty-four-hour town, and things never shut down."

It's important to mention that Don told me Arnie did not play the drums during this trip. He couldn't recall the exact reason, but at that time, Arnie had not been playing drums for very long. Someone may have decided they needed a more experienced drummer. Instead, the drumming duties were shared by Wynn Stewart's drummer and a hotel staff drummer.

The first few shows went well. Don played bass and sang tenor for Donny, while Gary played lead guitar and provided third-part harmony on some songs. Wynn Stewart's band, impressed by Donny's musicianship, often joined him on stage during parts of the show. Frequently, Donny would step away from the microphone to play the steel guitar, allowing Don to take over as the lead singer.

About a week into their engagement, someone from the club approached Gary to ask about his age. At just eighteen years old, Gary was too young to perform, as Nevada law required musicians to be at least twenty-one to play in clubs where gambling was allowed. This situation ended Gary's involvement in the show. Fortunately, no one asked to see Don's ID, since he wouldn't turn 21 for another two months. Gary stuck around for a day or two, but feeling unhappy about being sidelined, he decided to go home. Since Arnie's car was used for the trip, he had no choice but to go along, and Red Dog joined them as well. Given that they hadn't earned any money while traveling across the country and hadn't yet been paid, they had only around $20 to fund their journey home.

Donny could have cashed a stolen check, but for reasons unknown, he chose not to. Instead, Donny and Don gave Gary a song they had co-written titled "Somewhere Between the Window and the Phone." They told him that if he, Arnie, and Red Dog could make it to Oklahoma City, he should find record producer L.D. Allen and try to sell him the song.

Gary, Arnie, and Red Dog set off on their journey and, after twenty hours on the road, they coasted into Oklahoma City on fumes. They parked their car in a hotel parking lot, took a couple of hours to rest, and then started inquiring at local clubs about L.D. Allen. It didn't take long for them to locate him. Allen purchased the song for fifty dollars and a tank of gas, which was enough to get them back home to Greenfield.

It is worth mentioning that Wanda Jackson recorded the song under the shortened title "Between the Window and the Phone" in 1965. The song was released as a single, but it did not chart.

Meanwhile, back in Las Vegas, Donny and Don continued performing nightly to crowds of weary-eyed gamblers. This experience was a great learning opportunity for Don, as it was his first time on stage with a band made up entirely of seasoned professional musicians. By this point, Donny had been singing professionally for several years and had developed a relaxed stage presence that Don aspired to emulate.

They were paid once a week, but after the fourth week, they stopped receiving their paychecks. Don asked Donny what was going on, and Donny said that he did not know what was going on, but they were working on it, though he did not clarify who "they" were. The truth was that Donny had taken an advance on their last week's pay, but instead of paying Don, he was using the money to gamble at the casino and was losing badly.

"I was sending most of my paycheck home, so I was broke," Don recalled. "The maid left a roll of nickels in the room every day to encourage you to play the slots. That's all I had. For a week, I lived on a couple of loaves of bread and a gallon of Karo syrup, the clear kind that babies eat. I thought I was going to starve."

After their final show on December 23, Donny admitted that he had gambled away their pay. He explained that he had been trying to win them a bonus. Donny promised to repay Don for the money he owed, but he never followed through.

Low on funds and eager to get home for Christmas, Donny used a stolen check to purchase airline tickets for himself and Don. They flew from Las Vegas to Chicago, as no flights were available to Dayton, Cincinnati, or Columbus due to the Christmas rush. Don's brother-in-law, Cork McCune, picked them up from the airport and drove them to Ohio.

Although Don did not receive his full pay, he credits that trip to Las Vegas with convincing him that he could make a living playing music, and that became his goal.

After the holidays, Donny and the band, now featuring Arnie on drums and Jimmy Crawford from Columbus on steel guitar, embarked on a tour of nightclubs and honky-tonks across the country. While there are no records detailing all the cities they performed in, Don stated that they played numerous shows in and around Columbus. The *Greenfield Daily Times* published a story on January 18, 1962, noting that they had just completed a week-long engagement at the Golden Nugget nightclub in Columbus. The article also mentioned a show on January 20 at the Pan Theater in Portsmouth, Ohio, followed by a booking in Oklahoma City, a mid-February performance in Albuquerque, New Mexico, and a show on May 8 in Columbus at Lockbourne Air Force Base, which was likely the tour's last stop. Additionally, they appeared in Greenfield on February 14 at the McClain High School Auditorium as last-minute additions to a benefit show for the Greenfield Police Department, co-headlined by Tex Ritter and Smiley Burnette.

Due in part to the payola scandal*** gripping the music industry in the late 1950s and early 1960s, Donny's solo career was at a standstill. After finishing the tour, he returned to Nashville in early May to look for a job. Don, Arnie, Jimmy Crawford, and cousin Joe Adams, formed the Adams Boys Band. They performed at nightclubs throughout central and southern Ohio, primarily in Dayton and Columbus.[1]

Meanwhile, Gary, brimming with enthusiasm after his first extended time on the road, followed Donny to Nashville in pursuit of his dream.

---

1. *** The payola scandal was a music industry controversy where record labels paid DJs to heavily play certain records, artificially creating hits. New artists suffered fallout because station managers instructed DJs to play only songs from established stars to protect their stations from accusations of impropriety.*

PART TWO

The George Jones Years

Coal Shed Publishing

Chapter 3

Gary Lights the Match

Gary was interviewed by Paul Leslie for his podcast, *The Paul Leslie Hour*, in an episode that aired on January 3, 2020. During the interview, Gary claimed that he went to Nashville right after he "got out of school." However, this statement is inaccurate; Gary actually quit school at least a year before traveling to Nashville. This misconception may stem from his age, he was in his late 70s at the time and had many memories to recall.

In reality, Gary went to Nashville shortly after returning home from the tour with Donny. He borrowed $20.00 from his mother and told her that if things didn't work out, he would likely head to Detroit to find a job in one of the many automotive factories.

When Gary arrived in Nashville, he met Donny at Tootsie's Orchid Lounge, the most popular spot in town for singers, musicians, and songwriters at that time. Donny informed Gary that they would both be working for George Jones.

It turned out that George had called Tootsie's looking for Donny, and, coincidentally, Donny was there.

According to Gary, George told Donny he needed a steel guitar player and a lead guitar player. Donny answered that he could play steel and that a young guy from Ohio was coming down who could play lead. George agreed and sent Donny enough travel money for both of them to join him on the road.

Gary's reaction was likely a mix of surprise and excitement. At that time, George Jones was the number-one country singer in America, and his band, the Jones Boys, was considered one of the best in Nashville, alongside Ray Price's Cherokee Cowboys. Gary told Paul Leslie that he thought to himself, "Man, this is going to be easy."

In his 1998 best-selling autobiography, *I Lived to Tell It All*, George offered a different version of events. He stated that he met and hired Gary at Tootsie's, where Gary had gone to seek a job in the music industry. George recounted, "I met Gary Adams that night when he walked into the joint (Tootsie's), his first stop after graduating from high school." He also mentioned that he "hired Gary based on the recommendation of Johnny Paycheck." According to George, Donny had sent Gary to Tootsie's because he knew George would be there and that George had an upcoming show in New Mexico. George claimed he gave Gary $100 for him and Donny to travel to New Mexico.

Don told me he had never read George's book and was unfamiliar with George's version of the story. However, he mentioned that Gary always claimed he met Donny at Tootsie's and that Donny had already secured them jobs. Based on this information, I am inclined to believe Gary's account of events.

In his book, George quotes Gary as saying, "The tickets for the two of us cost $85. We had $15 left to live on for two days. The first night on the train, Johnny (Donny) got drunk. He was into karate at the time, and the next thing I knew, I heard a scream and a crashing of glass. He had put his hand through a window in the men's room."

Gary continued, "We had to get off the train and let a doctor sew up his hand, and that took the rest of our money. In all, it took three days to get out there, and we nearly starved to death because we had no money. Johnny (Donny) sobered up and told George that he had fallen down."

There is no mention in the book of how Donny played steel guitar with stitches in, presumably, his dominant right hand.

Regardless of the specifics, the reality is that Gary Adams, at just 19 years old, was now the lead guitarist for George Jones, the top country singer in all the land. Rounding out the Jones Boys were Donny on steel guitar, Gary Prawl on bass, Glen Davis on drums, and Georgie Riddle on rhythm guitar and background vocals. This opportunity would pave the way for outcomes that would ultimately shape the lives of the Notorious Adams Boys.

It is difficult to determine with absolute certainty the date and location of Gary's first show as lead guitarist for the Jones Boys. Based on George's claim that he had an upcoming show in New Mexico and the newspaper advertisements that confirmed his performances there from mid-May to late June, it is reasonable to conclude that Gary's first show took place on Wednesday, May 16, 1962, at 8:00 PM at the National Guard Armory in Hobbs, New Mexico, with George as the headliner and Skeeter Davis, among others, also performing.

On June 21, George Jones and the Jones Boys performed for more than 4,000 fans in Albuquerque, New Mexico, at an event called the "Shower of Stars." Other artists who participated in the show included Johnny Cash, Patsy Cline, Don Gibson, and Johnny Western.

Throughout the remainder of 1962, they toured across the United States and Canada. Notable performances included an appearance on August 25 at the famous Cabaret in Bandera, Texas; a show on September 9 at the Kentucky State Fair in Louisville, where they performed for an estimated crowd of over 20,000; a show on October 20 at the popular Cain's Ballroom in Tulsa, Oklahoma; a performance on November 9 in Nashville during Country Music Week; and a four-night engagement at Genova's Chestnut Inn in Kansas City from November 14 to 17. Additionally, the Jones Boys, without George, performed a scheduled New Year's Eve show at the Longhorn Club in Wichita Falls, Texas.

When the calendar flipped to 1963, George had a new bus and it was quickly put to good use. Leaving Nashville, the band drove south to Texas, where they reunited with George and performed several shows. Their first performance was on January 12 in San Antonio. Afterward, they headed to California, playing in Sacramento on January 16 and in Oakland on January 18. They then traveled back across the country for a series of shows in Kansas, Iowa, and Nebraska, before crossing the border into Canada, where they played several shows from February 2 to February 11.

On Sunday, March 3, there was a benefit show at Memorial Hall in Kansas City for disc jockey "Cactus" Jack Call's widow. Call had been killed in a car wreck on January 25. Appearing on the show, in addition to George Jones and the Jones Boys, were Roy Acuff, Billy Walker, Ralph Emery, Cowboy Copas, Hawkshaw Hawkins, and Patsy Cline.

There were three scheduled performances: 2:00 PM, 5:15 PM, and 8:15 PM. The Jones Boys were the only band performing, so they accompanied all the performers, including George.

After the show, Patsy stopped by their dressing room and in a cheerful voice said, "Bye, guys. PC checking out."

Gary had no idea it would be the last time he would see Patsy Cline.

Tragically, Patsy, along with Cowboy Copas, Hawkshaw Hawkins, and pilot Randy Hughes, were killed when their small plane crashed in bad weather on their return trip to Nashville near Camden, TN, on March 5.

After a show in Redding, CA, on March 29, George and the Jones Boys took off on an overnight bus ride to Salem, OR, for a performance there on March 30. Around 3:00 AM, while everyone was asleep, the bus driver swerved to avoid hitting a car, causing the bus to go off the road and throwing everyone from their bunks. George sustained a mild chest fracture and was kept in the hospital overnight for observation. Gary and the others only suffered bumps and bruises and were treated and released. Despite the accident, Georgie Riddle and the band performed that evening at the Armory Auditorium in Salem. However, the next five shows in Portland, OR, and in Miami, Orlando, and Pensacola, FL, were canceled to give George time to recover. The new bus was completely demolished in the accident.

Chapter 4

Don Joins the Jones Boys

In mid-April 1963, encouraged by Buddy Emmons and Darrell McCall, Gary decided to leave George and join Ray Price's band, The Cherokee Cowboys. He didn't need much persuasion, as Price was a major country music superstar, and Gary had long aspired to play alongside Buddy Emmons, who was highly respected as a musician and already recognized as one of the top steel guitarists in country music history. Don described Emmons as Gary's "hero," stating that "Gary would do almost anything to play with Buddy."

At first, Gary did not inform George about his plans, but he did tell Don and Donny. Together, the three of them vowed to find a way to get Don into the band.

Gary planned his final performance with the Jones Boys for May 1 at the Derby Festival Show in Louisville, Kentucky. This annual event, sponsored by the tobacco company Philip Morris Incorporated, took place in the days leading up to the Kentucky Derby at the Fairgrounds Coliseum and was free to the public. The 1963 show featured an impressive lineup, including George Jones, Ray Price, Faron Young, Skeeter Davis, Minnie Pearl, Tex Ritter, and Carl Butler.

April was a busy month for the band. They performed in several package shows across the United States and Canada, sharing the stage with Johnny Cash. Ray Price and The Cherokee Cowboys were also part of the lineup, along with Minnie Pearl, Grandpa Jones, and others. On April 28, they had a show in Chicago at the Arie Crown Theatre, after which they enjoyed three days off.

After the show in Chicago, Gary and Donny went to Greenfield. Don mentioned that he wasn't certain, but it was likely that Larry "Red Dog" Adams had driven to Chicago and then given them a ride back to Greenfield.

While in Greenfield, Gary, Donny, and Don came up with a straightforward plan to get Don into the band. Don would accompany Donny and Gary to Louisville and join them backstage. At a certain moment, Gary would inform George, in front of Donny and Don, that he was quitting the Jones Boys to work for Ray Price. Faced with the possibility of losing his lead guitarist, George would be caught off guard.

Donny would quickly propose that he take Gary's place as the lead guitarist, while Don could be hired to play bass. He felt confident that their plan was foolproof, and everyone agreed to move forward with it.

For Don, the opportunity to play for George Jones, the top country vocalist in America, was a dream come true, both musically and financially. At the time, the Jones Boys were earning ninety dollars a week, which was a decent salary then.

On May 1, the trio set out for Louisville. When they arrived at the venue, Donny and Gary went backstage to get dressed and prepare for their performance. Meanwhile, Don stayed behind, chatting with acquaintances and passing the time.

Just before going on stage, Gary approached George to inform him that he would be going to work for Ray Price.

George appeared taken aback by the news, but he quickly replied, "Well then, I suppose you're wearing the wrong uniform, aren't you?"

Donny suggested, "George, I can switch to lead guitar while Don plays bass."

George said, "Alright, you'd better get dressed." Just like that, Don officially became a member of the Jones Boys.

Gary removed his uniform and handed it to Don.

Looking back, Don said, "John (Donny) told me he would get me into the band. I already knew what the plan was, but I wasn't sure if George would hire me. Even if he did hire me, I didn't think I would actually play that night. I was several inches taller than Gary, so the uniform didn't fit very well. The arms and legs were too short, which made me stick out in every direction. I wore the pants really low on my hips. I wasn't wearing cowboy boots, or it would have looked even worse. I eventually got a uniform that fit a few days later."

It is unclear why they chose to inform George about the news before the show rather than afterward. Perhaps Gary accidentally revealed it too early, or maybe they thought surprising George would encourage him to hire Don on the spot. If that was their intention, it certainly worked.

Don had no trouble performing at his first show that evening. He had been listening to George Jones on the radio for years and had played his songs numerous times in Paul Angel's basement and at various shows around Greenfield.

With Don joining the band as the bassist and Gary leaving, the Jones Boys lineup consisted of Don on bass, Donny on lead guitar, Glen Davis on drums, and Georgie Riddle on rhythm guitar and background vocals. Soon, Tony Farr would join the band to play steel guitar.

When I asked Don how it felt to play for George Jones, he said, "I was 22 years old, making 90 bucks a week, and I thought I was on top of the world."

After the show in Louisville, George Jones and the Jones Boys performed at Cobo Hall in Detroit on May 5 and at the VFW Auditorium in Greenville, Tennessee, on May 7. The Greenville concert attracted a full house of 1,200 fans, with many people turned away at the door. Following that, they headed to the East Coast, where they played a series of shows in Virginia and the Carolinas before heading to Texas.

As for Gary, Don mentioned that he might have played for Ray Price that night, but he could not recall for sure.

After the show, Gary boarded Price's bus as the newest member of the Cherokee Cowboys. Following their departure from Louisville, they performed in Syracuse, New York, at the War Memorial on May 3; Dayton, Ohio, at the Municipal Auditorium on May 4; and in Detroit at Cobo Hall on May 5, where, since George was performing there also, Gary reunited with Don for a few hours.

There aren't many stories about Gary's brief time with Ray Price and the Cherokee Cowboys. However, Diane McCall shared something interesting that Gary and her brother Darrell told her during a few days off when they were staying in Jamestown.

Diane recounted an incident that occurred while Price's bus was traveling along a highway in the Midwest. Gary, Darrell McCall, and Buddy Emmons got into an argument and began throwing their belongings out of the windows of the moving bus. For example, Gary tossed out his watch, Darrell threw out a cowboy hat, and Buddy followed by discarding a pair of boots. Why they did this remains a mystery. Perhaps they were trying to show off their supposed wealth, implying they could easily replace their items without a second thought. Who knows?

Gary's experience with Ray Price was invaluable. Performing alongside the renowned steel guitarist Buddy Emmons gave him the experience that propelled him into the ranks of country music's top guitarists. After about six months, though, Gary wanted to go back to George. Gary told Don that Price didn't allow much artistic expression on stage, insisting that his songs be played just like the record. George, on the other hand, did allow his band to experiment a little on stage. That was more Gary's style, so he called George, and George brought him back. His first show back with the Jones Boys was on October 11 in San Bernardino, CA, at the famous Swing Auditorium. I know that because Don told me he remembered exactly when it was. I asked Don how he remembered that.

Don's answer? "I don't know. I just do."

Don and Gary were together again, and both were feeling very happy.

Meanwhile, back in Greenfield, Arnie continued playing drums with local bands, gaining valuable experience that helped him advance to the next level. Soon, his big opportunity would arrive.

Chapter 5

The Hollywood Bowl

Starring Hurricane Shirley

B oth Adams Boys performed with George Jones at the famous Hollywood Bowl in Los Angeles, California, but not together. Gary took the stage there on June 15, 1962, followed by Don on June 22, 1963.

The 1962 show, advertised as the "1st Giant Folk Western Bluegrass Musical Spectacular," featured Johnny Cash as the headliner. It also included performances by George Jones and the Jones Boys (with Gary on lead guitar), Patsy Cline, Marty Robbins, Flatt & Scruggs, Don Gibson, Gene Autry, Mother Maybelle and the Carter Family, June Carter, Roger Miller, and Lorne Greene.

Sadly, I have been unable to find a recording of the 1962 show, and there is limited information available.

The 1963 show, which lacked an official name, featured Johnny Cash as the headliner. The lineup included George Jones and the Jones Boys, Faron Young, Flatt & Scruggs, The

Louvin Brothers, Mother Maybelle and the Carter Family, Grandpa Jones, June Carter, The Chuckwagon Gang, Loretta Lynn, Georgie Riddle, The Plainsmen Quartet, and special guest Walter Brennan.

On the day of the show, Cash was struggling with a case of strep throat, and his voice reflected it. Despite the challenge, he delivered a solid, if not great, vocal performance.

George Jones and the Jones Boys were on stage for about 15 minutes and performed six songs, starting with "White Lightning" and ending with "She Thinks I Still Care."

Don played bass, and he may have provided background vocals, although it was most likely Georgie Riddle who handled that role. When Don joined the Jones Boys, Riddle was providing background vocals and playing rhythm guitar while Don only played bass. However, it wasn't long before Riddle left, and Don took over the background vocals.

The complete 1963 show is available on YouTube and is definitely worth a listen.

While interviewing Don about their appearances at the Hollywood Bowl, the topic of groupies came up. I asked him if there were women who followed singers and bands across the country, hoping to meet them. He explained that there were no women following them around the country. However, there were women in certain cities who kept close tabs on who was coming to perform and when. "They'd hang around the hotel. Usually at the pool or in the bar," he said.

Don reiterated that most of these women were simply fans hoping to get an autograph or a photo with their favorite star. However, a few had more intimate aspirations.

"We'd be in some cities several times a year," he said. "And the same women would be hovering around every time we showed up. Everybody knew who they were. We gave some of them nicknames like The Jacksonville Dog, The Bronc,

The Phantom, Miss Palomino, Aunt Wanda, and Hurricane Shirley."

Hurricane Shirley made an appearance at the Hollywood Bowl show in 1963.

According to Don, Hurricane Shirley showed up and talked her way into the backstage dressing room area before the show started.

"What did she look like?" I asked.

"Redhead. Big tits. Looked a little like Sophia Loren," Don answered.

"Wow! What was she doing there? Just watching the show?"

Don laughed. "She blew her way through everyone on the show just to get to Faron Young."

"Including you?" I asked.

"Nope. I wasn't there," Don answered.

"Where were you?"

"I must have been getting dressed for the show."

"You missed it, huh? I bet that pissed you off."

"Nope," he said. "I wasn't into that stuff."

I didn't press the issue any further.

Chapter 6

Road Incidents

Pull This Car Over

D on shared a funny story that occurred sometime in 1963 while Gary was away playing for Ray Price:

We were driving along somewhere in Iowa or Missouri, or somewhere like that. George was driving with me and John (Donny) up front. Hal Rugg and Glen Davis were riding in the back. It was late afternoon, four o'clock, maybe. Anyway, we were driving along, and George and John got into an argument. They were always arguing about something. It got kind of heated, and John said to George, "Pull this car over!"
George said, "What for?"

John looked at George and said, "Because, I'm going to whip your goddamned ass!"

Well, George pulled the car over, and John opened the door and jumped out. When he did, George took off, leaving him standing there. We drove about a mile and came upon this root beer stand at the edge of some little town. George pulled into it, and we all got out and ordered a root beer. About thirty minutes later, here came John walking up the road. We were all laughing at John, and he wasn't even mad. He was laughing too, and he walked up to George, shook his hand, and said, "You got me, didn't you?"

Fireworks and MLK Jr.

In 1963 or 1964, the Jones Boys were traveling between shows somewhere in Arkansas when they spotted a fireworks stand at the edge of a small town. Gary, who was driving, quickly pulled the car over to the shoulder to check it out. After purchasing a variety of items, including bottle rockets, Roman candles, firecrackers, and smoke bombs, they got back in the car. This time, Don took the wheel as they continued on their journey.

As they drove along, they passed the time lighting their fireworks with their cigarettes and tossing them out the windows toward mailboxes, road signs, fence posts, trees, and empty fields. At one point, a firecracker exploded on the floorboard at Don's feet, nearly causing him to run the car off the road, and eliciting a stream of profanities and threats of violence towards the perpetrator.

Soon, they arrived at a ferry landing on the Mississippi River at a crossing between Arkansas and Mississippi. The ferry had just launched from the Mississippi shore, so it would be several minutes before it got to the Arkansas side to transport Don and the boys to the other side.

Don put the car in park and stepped outside to smoke a cigarette. A few of the other guys got out to take a bathroom break or stretch their legs, while a couple more continued launching bottle rockets and Roman candles into a large field.

After a few minutes, they saw the ferry approaching, so they all got back into the car.

As they waited, a cloud of smoke began drifting across the road.

"I turned and looked to see where the smoke was coming from and saw that the field next to the car was on fire," Don recalled. "It was burning in four or five small patches and looked like it was starting to spread. It was pretty dry, and evidently the fireworks had set the field on fire. I thought, *holy shit, we have to get out of here.*"

The ferry docked, and as a procession of vehicles began passing the Jones Boys' car, smoke continued to drift across the road, and the small fires were clearly visible.

Don continued, "Two or three cars passed by us, followed by a delivery truck or something like that. Behind the truck were two more cars, both filled with Black men in suits. When the second car passed, I made eye contact with the man sitting in the back seat. I recognized him immediately from having seen him on the news. It was Martin Luther King Jr."

What are the chances of passing just a few feet from Dr. Martin Luther King Jr. while on a highway in the middle of nowhere, especially after you had just set a field on fire? The answer is very close to zero. Yet, there they were.

"There was only one car behind King's car, and that was a police cruiser. I guess he was following him (MLK), and either didn't notice the smoke or didn't care because he slowed down but didn't stop. We were the only car going the other direction, so we got loaded up, and they took off for the other side."

I asked Don the obvious question, "What about the fire?"

"We watched it burn from the ferry. It was smoky as hell."

Don made them all put the fireworks away, and he did not stop driving until they were far away from the landing.

It's hard to be precise, but it appears that Arnie joined the Jones Boys on or around November 1, 1963, with his first show being on November 12 in Austin, TX, at Memorial Auditorium.

I'm basing this on three pieces of information: First of all, I heard Arnie mention in an interview that he was on the road with George Jones when President John F. Kennedy was assassinated on November 22, 1963. Second, Don told me that drummer Glen Davis quit after a show in Canada and that Arnie's first show was in Texas. They played in Toronto, ON, on October 27 before taking a break. It makes sense that Davis would have left at the end of a tour rather than in the middle if he left on good terms. And third, the first show they played after the break was in Austin, and Don told me that Arnie started at the beginning of a tour.

Chapter 7

The Buddy Emmons Incident

On February 2, 1964, George Jones and the Jones Boys performed at the iconic Cain's Ballroom in Tulsa, Oklahoma. Ray Price was originally scheduled to perform, but due to scheduling conflicts, he was unable to make it. George's booking agent contacted him about a week prior and asked if he could fill in, as George would be finishing a tour in Amarillo on February 1 and didn't have any other bookings until February 7 in Jessup, Maryland. George agreed, as this would provide him with an additional payday and it didn't require traveling far out of his way.

The show was scheduled for 8:00 PM, and the band arrived well in advance. They set up their equipment before heading to a nearby restaurant for a meal. After eating, they returned to Cain's to prepare for the performance.

According to Don, they had bought a large amount of marijuana in Amarillo the day before. After getting dressed, Gary, Arnie, and Buddy Emmons decided to smoke some of it. It is unclear what Don was doing to pass the time, but apparently, he was not smoking marijuana.

George, who was traveling separately, arrived 30 minutes before showtime and, as per his usual routine, had a couple of drinks to get settled in.

A full house gathered to enjoy the show and dance the night away. As is typical of dance hall performances, the event was divided into three sessions, each lasting about 30 minutes, with 15 to 20 minute breaks between them.

The show started, and the first session went well. During the break, Gary, Arnie, and Buddy stepped outside and smoked the rest of their marijuana, leaving all three quite high.

"You see," Don explained, "back in those days, getting caught with marijuana could land you in prison for years. So whenever we bought some, we would smoke it all at once to get rid of it. I'm talking about an entire Prince Albert can."

After the break, they began the second session. Once again, everything went as planned until George left the band-stand. At that moment, the band started playing "Jonesy," the instrumental piece that had become their theme song, signaling the start of intermission. As the music came to an end, Buddy's bar, the smooth, steel object used to press against and slide over the strings of a steel guitar, slipped from his hand. It flew through the air and landed on the dance floor, sliding beneath a table where two couples were seated.

Don and Gary witnessed the incident and burst out laughing, which only made Buddy, already frustrated, furious.

Buddy stepped down from the bandstand and walked across the dance floor to retrieve his bar from under the table where the two couples were sitting. As he approached, one of the men nudged the bar with his foot, pushing it out from under the table and into the open. This irritated Buddy, and he exchanged words with the man before picking up his bar and heading back to the bandstand.

By that time, Don and Gary had filled Arnie in on what had happened, and the three Adams brothers started teasing Buddy per the usual standard.

Angrily, Buddy glared at the brothers and, without saying a word, packed up his equipment and left with two women that he had been flirting with earlier, who were sitting at a table near the stage.

"We didn't know where he was going," Don recalled. "He just sacked his stuff up and left with two women from the audience that he had been talking to. He wouldn't tell us anything. He just left. We found out later that the two women took him to the airport, and Buddy went back to Nashville."

With Buddy gone, Don called Sonny Curtis to take over on steel guitar. Sonny joined the band a few days later in Jessup, Maryland.

When they got back to Nashville the next day, Don, Gary, and Arnie went to Buddy's house and asked him why he had left.

"You know why I left," Buddy said. "You greased my bar and made it slip out of my hand."

Don said that no one had greased Buddy's bar. "We had been playing all night without any issues, and then suddenly Buddy lost his bar. Are we supposed to believe it was because we greased it? We didn't have any grease on stage with us. That's ridiculous. The real reason is that he couldn't hold onto his bar because he was stoned."

A year later, Buddy rejoined the Jones Boys in Houston to perform with them during a live recording at Dance Town USA. Everyone had a good laugh about the incident, but Buddy continued to insist that his bar had been greased. "He believed until the day he died that we had greased his bar," Don said.

Despite the incident, Don, Gary, and Arnie remained friends with Buddy over the years, frequently performing on stage together into the 2000s.

Chapter 8

Lighting Up the Big Apple

Big Dumb Arnie

On February 13, 1964, televisions in Greenfield and across America were tuned to *The Jimmy Dean Show* to watch George Jones and the Jones Boys appear as guests. George sang three songs, "Your Heart Turned Left (And I Was On the Right), "She Thinks I Still Care," and "Who Shot Sam?" Don is featured prominently as he sings tenor with George, while Arnie and Gary can clearly be seen in the background.

The best part of the show, though, is when Jimmy Dean asked George to introduce the members of his band.

George begins by turning to his right and introducing the steel guitar player, Sonny Curtis. He then turns to Don and says, "And here on the bass is Don Adams." Turning to Arnie, George says, "The boy on the drums is a brother to Don. His name is Big Dumb Arnie Adams." It's interesting to note that before George introduces him, Arnie smiles like he knows that George is going to say something funny. Arnie's face is hidden after George introduces him, so his further reaction is unknown. I suspect he got quite the kick out of it, though. Gary, however, has a wide smile on his face, clearly amused by George's comment. When George turns towards Gary and says, "And back here on the guitar is the young Adams brother of the family. His name is Gary Adams." Gary's smile fades, and he shifts nervously back and forth on his feet, looking side to side. George then introduces fiddle player Charlie Justice to end the segment.

The show is available on YouTube, and I encourage everyone to watch it.

Madison Square Garden

On May 16 and 17, 1964, George Jones and the Jones Boys were part of what was considered, at the time, the most important country music show ever held. The site was Madison Square Garden in New York, and the show was billed as the National Country Music Cavalcade of Stars. It was the first country music show ever held at Madison Square Garden.

Also on the show were Ernest Tubb, Buck Owens, Webb Pierce, Bill Monroe, Bill Anderson, Stonewall Jackson, Skeeter Davis, Porter Wagoner, and Leon McCaulife. The master of ceremonies was Ralph Emery.

Because of union rules, the show was supposed to end no later than 11:30 PM. Therefore, each performer was restricted to two songs. George was scheduled to go on next to last, right before Buck Owens, who was closing the show. Well, George sang "White Lightning" and another song and just kept right on going, singing a total of five songs before he was literally dragged from the stage kicking and yelling.

The Jones Boys were trying to get off the stage and got tangled up with Owens' band, The Buckaroos, who were trying to get plugged in.

Owens barely got through his two songs in time, and the show ended at precisely 11:29:40 PM

Chapter 9

I Just Lost My Favorite Girl

Early in 1964, George's manager, Pappy Daily, recognizing Don's potential as a solo artist, signed Don to his record label, D Records. Eager to get into the studio, Don approached his friend, Jimmy Day, and asked for his help in selecting a song to record. Day was happy to help Don find a song and offered him one he had written a year or two earlier called "I Just Lost My Favorite Girl." Don liked the song and decided to record it. There was one problem, though. Don and Jimmy Day were signed to different publishing companies, and under the rules of the time, a singer could only record songs published by the same company he was signed to.

Day devised a workaround, though. Because no one outside of him and Don knew it existed, he told Don he would give him the song, and Don could claim it as his own as long as he didn't tell anyone it was really Day's. Don agreed, and

Day transferred the writer's credit to him with nothing more than a promise and a handshake.

Don took the song to Pappy Daily, and Daily agreed to record it for Don, with Don credited as the songwriter. The B side of the record was a song named "You Introduced Me to the Blues."

Daily sent records to DJs at country music stations across the country, and "I Just Lost My Favorite Girl" quickly went to Number 1 or 2 in several major markets, including Memphis, Houston, Atlanta, Cincinnati, Kansas City, and more. The problem was that D Records had no distribution outside of radio stations, so record stores, which desperately wanted the record, were unable to get them to sell. Thus, "I Just Lost My Favorite Girl" failed to chart even though it was very popular on the radio.

Recognizing the problem, Daily transferred Don's recording contract to Musicor Records, the same label that George was signed to. Musicor halfheartedly distributed the record to record stores in select parts of the country, but it did not reach the numbers needed to get it on the charts. After a couple of months, stations moved on to new songs, and interest in "I Just Lost My Favorite Girl" fizzled.

It's worth noting that Don never revealed to anyone that Jimmy Day, not he, was the true writer of the song. This remained a secret until Day passed away in 1999. After that, Don felt it was okay to share the truth, so he did. However, "I Just Lost My Favorite Girl" is still credited to Don Adams to this day.

Don went on to release three more records with Musicor, "Kill Me with Kindness" and "Big Town Baby" in 1965, and "Heartaches Morning, Noon, and Night" in 1966. None charted, but "Big Town Baby" garnered significant airplay on radio stations in certain markets.

Chapter 10

Take Him to Jail

In mid-1964, George Jones and the Jones Boys performed at the famous Cabaret Dance Hall in Bandera, Texas, located about 50 miles north of San Antonio.

The band, including George, arrived a couple of hours before their performance. While Don and the other band members set up the stage and got dressed, George sat alone at a table in the empty dance hall, sipping Canadian whisky.

As showtime approached and the crowd started to trickle in, Don and the band conducted their sound check. Meanwhile, two young women joined George at his table and began chatting with him. Anticipating potential trouble, Don approached the table and reminded George that it was time to get dressed and prepare for the show.

George casually said, "Donald, I'd like you to meet Dixie and Trixie. They're old friends of mine, and they've been looking forward to meeting you." In truth, the women's names were not Dixie and Trixie, nor were they George's old friends. It is unclear if they were eager to meet Don.

After persistent persuasion from Don, George, still clutching his bottle of whiskey, finally excused himself and followed Don to the dressing room. He got dressed and seemed ready to proceed with the show.

The Jones Boys kicked off the show right on time. Don sang three or four songs, followed by an instrumental number. After that, he performed another song or two. Then it was time to introduce George, who was standing behind a curtain, out of view of the audience but visible to the band. Don spoke into his microphone, "Thank you, ladies and gentlemen. Now we would like to introduce our boss to you. America's number-one Country and Western singer. George Jones!"

The band started playing the intro to "White Lightning," and the crowd erupted in cheers. Couples made their way to the dance floor, while others gathered near the bandstand for a better view of George. However, there was one issue: George did not come out. Don recalled, "I turned and looked at George, and he was staring at me with a scowl on his face. I knew what was going on. He wasn't going to come out."

The band continued playing their introduction, and once more, Don introduced George: "Ladies and gentlemen, please welcome George Jones!"

Don continued, "I was looking right at him when I introduced him for the second time. He just flipped me the bird and stayed right where he was. At that point, I told the crowd that George would be right out, but while we were waiting, I'd sing another song. We kicked off another song, and out of the corner of my eye, I saw something coming at me. George threw his whisky bottle at me, and it went sailing right past my head. I looked over at him, and he was peeking out from behind the curtain and flipping off some people in the audience."

I asked Don what the crowd's reaction was at that point. He said, "Most of them were just sitting there, wondering what the hell was going on. Others were laughing because George Jones was giving them the finger."

Don finished his song and made one last effort to coax George out. The crowd was growing increasingly frustrated, so Don told the band that he would give George one final introduction. If George didn't come out this time, they would quickly pack everything up and leave before the situation escalated.

"Ladies and gentlemen," Don announced, "It looks like the star of the show is ready to sing. Please give a big welcome to George Jones!"

As the band started playing "White Lightning," Don turned to see if George was coming out. To his relief, George walked up to the bandstand and began singing, "Well, in North Carolina, way back in the hills..." The crowd erupted with excitement.

"Drinking did not affect his ability to sing in those days. He was unpredictable when he was drunk, but his ability to sing a song wasn't affected," Don said.

Most dance hall shows usually featured three 30-minute sets with short breaks in between. However, during the show in Bandera, George continued drinking between the first and second sets and ultimately refused to come out for the third set. Consequently, the night ended early.

While the band packed up their gear and loaded it into the trailer, George had another drink. What happened next is the stuff of legends. Don recalled:

> I was loading our equipment into the trailer and
> talking to a deputy sheriff who had been at the

show. I had my back turned and was kind of leaning into the trailer, moving stuff around a little. Behind me, I heard gravel crunching like someone was walking up on me really fast. I turned around and saw George coming at me with his fists doubled up and this big scowl on his face. I let him get within three feet or so, then I swung the trailer door out towards him, and it hit him square in the face. He hit the ground like a sack of rocks. Flat on his back, out like a light. The deputy sheriff I had been talking to walked over, and we both stood there looking down at George. We stood there for a few seconds, and he finally said to me, "What do you want me to do with him, Don?"
I said, "Take him to jail."
So, he drug George over to his cruiser, opened the door, and slung him on the back seat. We all watched as George headed to jail, then we (Don, Gary, Arnie, and Sonny Curtis) got in the car and drove to Greenfield.

A few days later, Don received a call from George, who informed him that he had been fired along with Gary and Arnie. About an hour later, George called again to offer him his job back.

According to Don, George fired them at least a dozen times. "He would fire us for a day and then rehire us. Sometimes he would forget he'd fired us, and we would just act like it never happened. It didn't mean anything."

I asked Don how slamming the trailer door in George's face and sending him to jail affected their relationship afterward. He replied, "It didn't have any effect at all. We never talked about it. It was as if it never happened."

Chapter 11

Driving George to Greenfield

Afunny thing happened late one night in the summer of 1964. Diane McCall and her mother were watching the eleven o'clock news at their home in Jamestown, OH, when they saw a car pull into their driveway. Not knowing who might be coming to their house at such a late hour, Mrs. McCall went to the window to check. A man got out of the car and walked toward the house. Mrs. McCall turned to Diane and said, "It's George Jones!"

Both ladies went to the door, and Mrs. McCall said, "Hello, George. To what do we owe the honor?"

George apologized for arriving unannounced at such an hour and told them that he was driving to Greenfield from a show in Dayton, adding, "I was wondering if the girl who lives here could drive my car the rest of the way to Greenfield. I'm really tired, and my drummer is asleep in the back seat. I just don't think I can make it to Greenfield."

The trio then walked out to the car, and when Diane looked in the back seat, she saw Arnie lying there, not asleep but passed out drunk.

Mrs. McCall hesitated, understandably, not convinced that allowing Diane, who was around 19 at the time, to drive two men 35 miles to Greenfield at eleven o'clock at night was a good idea. But she had met George before when he stopped by with the Adams Boys on a couple of occasions, and she trusted him to take care of Diane.

"Diane, do you think you can drive these guys to Greenfield?" Mrs. McCall asked.

Diane, who didn't have a driver's license, said, "Yes, I think I could do that okay."

George promised Mrs. McCall that he would take care of Diane and see to it that someone brought her safely home.

Diane got herself dressed, then got behind the wheel of George's Cadillac with instructions to drive them to Paul Angel's house in Greenfield. George then leaned against the passenger side door and fell asleep, while Arnie remained passed out in the backseat.

Diane was pretty sure she knew how to get to Greenfield, so with both hands on the wheel, off she went.

Arriving in Greenfield, Diane had no trouble finding Paul's house as she had been there a few times before with Gary. George woke up when they arrived, and after rousing Arnie, he thanked Diane, and the two men headed into Paul's basement, where people were playing music. True to his word, George sent someone outside to drive Diane back to Jamestown, and she arrived home safely.

Diane discovered later that George didn't know for sure who lived at their house in Jamestown. He just recognized the house when he drove past and remembered that someone he knew lived there.

"They (George and the band) had picked up, or dropped off, Gary at the house on a few occasions when they were heading out or getting back from a tour. So, he figured whoever lived there might be able to get them to Greenfield." Diane said.

Chapter 12

The Teen Fair of Texas

The Teen Fair of Texas was a ten-day event held from June 5 to June 14, 1964, at the Joe Freeman Coliseum and its 176-acre fairgrounds in San Antonio, Texas. The fair aimed to celebrate the two million teenagers living in the Lone Star State.

Attractions included a Midway with rides, games, and food stands, as well as a queen pageant, sideshows, and various contests. Special events featured a hot rod show, a rodeo, a space exhibit, a display of military hardware, and a range of live entertainment and musical performances. The fair was sponsored by the Lions Club of Texas, and the proceeds were allocated to youth welfare projects throughout the state.

George Jones and the Jones Boys were scheduled to perform two shows each day at the fair: one at 2:00 PM and another at 8:00 PM. Following their performances, a quirky parade of acts would take place, featuring a troop of performing chimpanzees known as the Marquis Monkeys, comedic classical musicians Pompoff and Thedy, the acrobatic Amandis Troupe, and the fire-twirling Loundsberry Sisters. Only after these acts would the headlining performances begin.

- The scheduled headliners were as follows:
  June 5, 6, and 7: Bobby Vee with Myron Lee & The Caddies and Diane Renay
  June 8 and 9: Bobby Rydell and Linda Scott
  June 10, 11, and 12: Paul Peterson and Lesley Gore
  June 13 and 14: Johnny Tillotson, Claude King, and The Collins Kids

- Additionally, two British acts were included as "added attractions" to close the shows on June 6 through 9:
  June 6 and 7: the Rolling Stones
  June 8 and 9: Billy J. Kramer and the Dakotas.

A few months earlier, on February 7, the Beatles arrived in the United States, marking the start of the British Invasion. This cultural phenomenon led to a surge in popularity for all things British, particularly British rock music. The Beatles' success paved the way for other well-known British acts to come to America, and these bands gained immense popularity among American teenagers.

Recognizing this trend, the organizers of The Teen Fair of Texas decided to capitalize on it by booking two popular British bands: The Rolling Stones and Billy J. Kramer and The Dakotas. These two bands were advertised as "added attractions," allowing promoters to feature them as supporting acts in case they were not well received by the audience.

The fair opened on June 5, drawing a large crowd excited to watch George perform at the matinee show. George's voice was in excellent form, and reports indicated that he and the Jones Boys delivered a stellar performance. The variety acts that followed were also well received, with pretty Diane Renay a particular favorite among the men in the audience.

To conclude the show, Bobby Vee took the stage, and the young audience erupted with excitement. It was clear that Vee was the fair's main attraction, and he exceeded his fans' expectations. The evening performances were equally impressive, leading many to declare the first day a resounding success.

The following day, June 6, about an hour before George Jones and the Jones Boys were scheduled to take the stage for their matinee performance, The Rolling Stones arrived at the venue. They went to the large first-floor dressing room that George and his band had occupied the day before. Upon discovering that the dressing room was in use, someone from the Stones' small entourage, likely U.S. Tour Manager Bob Bonis, asked Don, "Why are you in this dressing room? This is our dressing room."

Don, unsure of who the men were, stood up and walked toward the door. "Who are you?" he asked.

Bonis, looking somewhat surprised, replied, "These are the Rolling Stones, the featured act today and tomorrow."

"George Jones is the star of this show." Don said. "Your dressing room is upstairs."

Arnie was sitting on a sofa, putting on his boots, when he made eye contact with the intruders. He pointed to the ceiling with his finger, indicating that they should go upstairs. There was a brief, uneasy silence before The Rolling Stones turned around and started up the steps to the second floor.

Once again, a large crowd gathered for George's matinee show, but this audience differed from what one might expect at an event marketed as a teen fair. Unlike the previous day's crowd, which was predominantly young, this audience was primarily older, made up of the same devoted fans who filled honky-tonks and dance halls across Texas whenever George performed. This shift in demographics was likely due to it being Saturday, a day when more people are off work compared to the previous day. The fans were not disappointed, as George delivered thirty-five minutes of hit after hit.

After finishing their performance, George and the band packed up their equipment, changed clothes, and headed out the door. As they climbed into his Cadillac for the short drive to the Holiday Inn, George proclaimed, "Last call for alkee-hol!" And off they went.

After returning to their hotel, everyone cleaned up, changed clothes, and had lunch. The Jones Boys gathered by the pool, while George chose to stay in his room and entertain a lady friend who had come to visit.

Two hours passed as the boys sunbathed, swam, and drank before Bobby Vee and his band joined them by the pool.

Don shared with me that, while talking to Bobby Vee and his band, they revealed that The Rolling Stones were almost booed offstage. The older members of the crowd criticized the band for their long hair, calling them girls. Even the young audience wasn't impressed; one girl yelled at them to "get out of Texas and go back to England." This news piqued everyone's curiosity, and even George was eager to see the Rolling Stones' second show after the guys told him about it.

When they returned to the Coliseum for the evening performance, Don and the band noticed Bobby Vee and his group standing outside, signing autographs for a crowd primarily made up of teenage girls. Curiosity got the better of Gary, and he decided to walk over to see what was happening, with Don following behind.

As they approached, several excited girls broke away from Bobby Vee and nearly knocked Gary and Don over, thrusting autograph books and pens in their faces. "I don't think they knew who we were," Don recalled. "They probably thought we were part of some rock band. Most of the girls looked to be between 12 and 16 years old. We signed a few autographs, but then I told Gary it was time to get out of there. So, we went back inside and watched from a window. Bobby Vee must have signed at least a hundred autographs."

After George's evening performance, the band was busy packing up when a disheveled-looking young man approached Sonny Curtis. The young man turned out to be Keith Richards, the guitarist for The Rolling Stones. He asked Sonny if he could borrow an amplifier for the Stones' show later that night. Although the Stones had brought their guitars to America, they relied on other bands or equipment rentals for the rest of their gear, such as drums, amps, and speakers. Richards had been using an amplifier from Bobby Vee's band, but was dissatisfied with it.

In response, Sonny offered Richards his Fender Brown Panel amplifier, which Richards gratefully accepted.

A much smaller crowd attended the evening show, which dwindled after George's performance and diminished further after Bobby Vee's. By the time The Rolling Stones took the stage, there were barely a thousand people in a venue that could seat nearly twelve thousand. George and the band decided to stay and watch the beginning of the Stones' performance to see them live and form their own opinions about the long-haired British rockers. Although George wasn't a fan of their music, he admired the Stones' stage presence and showmanship. Don, Arnie, and Gary were indifferent to their music, but they certainly had strong opinions about the band. "They stunk to high heaven," Don recalled. "They obviously hadn't showered since they got to San Antonio, and I'm not sure they even knew what deodorant was. Their clothes looked like they had been rolled up and used as a pillow or something. We weren't impressed. After two songs,

George had heard enough, so we got into the Cadillac and went back to the hotel."

The next morning, on June 7, George woke up with a hangover, so the Jones Boys left for the Coliseum without him to set up. George planned to take a taxi and would arrive about an hour later, just in time for his performance. That morning turned out to be quite eventful.

Sixty-one years later, I sat in Don Adams' living room in Greenfield, Ohio, as he recounted the story to me:

> When we got to the Coliseum, we got dressed and waited to go on. We was doing our sound check and Sonny's amp was popping and buzzing. Then it died and wouldn't come back on. After we finished setting up, we headed back to the dressing room and saw George in the hallway. Sonny told him that his amp was blown. George was hungover and in a bad mood already, so that made him even madder. About then, Keith Richards, Mick Jagger, and one of the others, Charlie Watts, the drummer, I think, walked towards us. Richards walked up to Sonny and said, "I accidentally blew up your amp," or something like that. We could barely understand them because of their accents. Anyway, Gary looked at him and said, "What did you say?"
> Richards said, "I said we blew the bloody amp up. I guess we were a little too loud. Sorry about that." Then he turned to walk away.
> Gary wasn't about to let that slide, so he grabbed Richards by the elbow to stop him and said, "Hold on now. You're going to have to pay for that."
> Richards looked kind of surprised and said, "Come on, mate, it was an accident."

That irritated Gary, so he took Richards by the arm and marched him into the dressing room, where George was. Gary told George, "This guy blew up Sonny's amp, and he needs to pay for it." George responded, "Well, hell yes, he's going to pay for it! Go upstairs and get some money. Sonny needs a goddamned amp!"

So, Gary walked Richards upstairs, still holding onto his arm. A few minutes later, he came down with a wad of cash."

I asked Don what Mick Jagger and the other guy, presumably Charlie Watts, did the whole time this incident was going on. "They didn't say a word. When Gary took Richards upstairs, they just followed behind," Don said.

Don was unsure what Gary said to get money for the amplifier, but knowing Gary's talent for delivering insults and one-liners, it was surely colorful.

Sonny had to use one of Bobby Vee's band's amplifiers for the show, possibly even the same amp that Richards had borrowed from Sonny before. The next morning, Sonny woke up early and rummaged through several pawn shops until he finally found an amplifier identical to the one he had lost.

In his autobiography, *I Lived to Tell It All*, George Jones shares a different version of the story. According to George, it was Mick Jagger, not Keith Richards, whom Gary confronted. He also claimed that Jagger took a one-hundred-dollar bill from his own pocket, which Gary then handed to George.

Don's version of the story makes more sense to me. Richards was the guitarist, and Jagger was the vocalist. It stands to reason that Richards would be more likely to need an amplifier.

On June 8, after finishing their performances, The Rolling Stones, Bobby Vee, and Diane Renay departed from San

Antonio. They were joined by Bobby Rydell, Linda Scott, and Billy J. Kramer and The Dakotas. The shows on June 8 and 9 went on as planned, but ticket sales had declined significantly. As a result, the organizers decided to cancel the scheduled headline acts for June 10-14. Instead, George Jones and the Jones Boys became the main attraction for the remaining shows. Although the crowds were small, George was compensated well, and they stayed at the Holiday Inn, where they enjoyed good meals and plenty of time by the pool. Overall, they felt content, almost as if they were on vacation.

Another notable incident involving the Adams Boy (one is never enough) took place during the ten-day fair. One afternoon, after lounging by the pool and enjoying more than a few drinks, Gary decided to head to his room. However, he was distracted by the sight of room service dishes left outside several rooms. Unable to resist the temptation, Gary thought it would be fun to use the ceramic plates as frisbees and throw them into the pool area.

Guests scattered as Gary hurled plates at them, first from ground level and then from the second floor. Meanwhile, Arnie and Don, who had been watching TV in their room, heard the sound of plates crashing onto the cement patio surrounding the pool. They stepped outside to see what was happening. Knowing it would be pointless to try to get Gary to stop, they simply watched and laughed until he ran out of plates and returned to his room.

The hotel manager was understandably upset. He presented George with a bill for the broken plates and warned him that he would evict him and the band if he did not pay it. Reluctantly, George settled the bill and nearly fired Gary over the incident. However, he ultimately decided against it, realizing that Gary's guitar skills were too valuable to lose on such short notice.

On the morning of June 15, George Jones and the Jones Boys left San Antonio to continue their seemingly endless journey across America, never to cross paths with The Rolling Stones again.

Chapter 13

Backstage Mischief

Donny Young has Dinner with Elvis

There has long been a persistent rumor that Johnny Paycheck once had dinner with Elvis Presley. I have heard this mentioned many times, particularly among Adams Boys fans. However, most people don't know any details; they simply recall hearing it somewhere and accept it as true.

I was one of those people until I asked Don Adams about it.

Don could not recall the exact year, but he said it happened when Johnny was performing as Donny Young, which would have been sometime before 1965. According to Don, the incident occurred in a hotel room in Los Angeles. At that time, the Adams Boys were performing with George Jones, and all three of them were present in the room. This narrows the timeframe down to between late 1963 and early 1965. Don explained that Donny was there as part of a package show alongside George and several other performers.

While hanging out in a hotel room a few hours before their show, Donny told the others, Don, Gary, Arnie, Sonny Curtis, and Charlie Justice, that he would be going to dinner with Elvis Presley later that evening after the show.

When asked how he received an invitation to dinner with Elvis Presley, Donny explained that Elvis's manager, Colonel Parker, had reached out to him a few weeks prior. He mentioned that Elvis was a fan of Donny's music and wanted to meet him. Since both were in Los Angeles that night, they planned to have dinner together after the show.

According to Don, that is when the alarm bells went off. The guys began asking probing questions, and Donny did his best to respond. At that moment, Gary sprang into action.

"We knew he was bullshitting," Don said. "He was starting to get mad because we were asking a lot of questions. He knew we didn't believe a word he was saying, but we never actually accused him of lying. Gary picked up the telephone and pretended to make a call."

That phone call went something like this:

Hello, Elvis? It's Donny.

Donny Young.

That's right. Young.

Elvis, I'm not able to go to dinner tonight. I have to...

Oh. Hello, Colonel Parker. I was just te...

It's Donny Young.

Donny Young. I...

Hello?

Hello?

Gary hung up the phone, and everyone in the room burst out in laughter except for Donny.

Donny stood up and headed for the door, but stopped halfway across the room. Looking first at Gary, then Don, and finally at Arnie, he said, "When I make it big one day, I'm leaving you motherfuckers behind!"

As far as Don knows, Donny/Johnny never did have dinner with Elvis.

Farrell Fills In

Sometime between Thanksgiving and Christmas in 1964, Arnie came down with a bad case of strep throat and was unable to travel.

While he was recuperating at home, his younger brother, Farrell, who was still in high school, took his place. Farrell, who considered himself a bass player first and foremost, filled in on drums admirably for seven or eight shows until Arnie could rejoin the band.

"I called Glen Davis, who was in Nashville at the time, and he was going to fill in, but something came up, so Farrell skipped school to help out," said Don.

Get Out of Buffalo

Shortly before Christmas in 1964, they performed in a package show at a small downtown theater in Buffalo, NY. According to Don, it was a smaller venue than they would usually play in a city of Buffalo's size. Although he couldn't recall the name of the theater, he remembered there was a coffee shop next door where he had the best cup of coffee he had ever tasted, just before the show.

Also on the show that night were Little Jimmy Dickens, Loretta Lynn, Melba Montgomery, and a local singer whose name Don could not remember.

George had flown into Buffalo and was actually at the theater when the band arrived, which was unusual, as George typically arrived just before showtime, assuming he showed up at all.

After setting up the stage, Don and the band, along with Loretta and Melba, went next door for coffee. Meanwhile, George sat in the dressing room, opened a bottle of Canadian whisky, and made a couple of calls from the payphone.

By the time the band returned, George was drunk, but he wasn't being troublesome. In fact, Don described him as being in a good mood. Little Jimmy Dickens had also arrived by then and was in the dressing room with George. Don said that he didn't recall Dickens being drunk.

The Jones Boys provided backing for all of the artists on the show, starting with the local singer, followed by Loretta Lynn, Melba Montgomery, and Little Jimmy Dickens in that order, before George came on to close the show. This schedule left George with some free time, which he used to continue drinking whisky.

According to Don, George was on edge when he took the stage and was fixated on a man sitting four or five rows back at the extreme right side of the stage. Evidently, George was under the impression that the man had said something off-color to Melba while she was on stage, which angered George. Don said,

George had a thing for Melba. She didn't feel the same about George, but she would flirt a little with him sometimes just to mess with him. She had a thing for Gary, though, and that bugged the hell out of George. But anyway, I never heard anyone say anything bad to Melba while she was on stage. I think she just told George that to get him riled up.

When George took the stage, he went through two or three songs, starting with "White Lightning," of course, before stopping to address the audience, thanking them for coming and hoping they enjoyed the show. Then he went off script, and that's when the trouble started.

George looked at the man he thought had insulted Melba and said, according to Don, "This next song goes out to that big fat son of a bitch sitting right out there," while pointing in his direction. "That's right," George continued, "I mean you."

With that, the band kicked off the song, "Big Harlan Taylor," and George changed the lyrics in the fifth line of the song from "I had a friend, a big fella, named Big Harlan Taylor," to "I knew a man, a big fat bastard, named Harlan Taylor."

"When the song ended, the guy yelled something at George, and he and George had a few words," said Don. "Then George said, 'If you have a problem with it, you can see Big Arnie after the show.' Arnie stood up and told the guy in the audience, 'Oh no. I don't have anything to do with this. There's your man right there,' (pointing at George)."

George continued throwing jabs at the man throughout the rest of the show, and when he left the stage, the police were waiting to meet him.

Don said, "The police told George that they wanted him to get in his car and get the hell out of Buffalo because he was liable to get killed if he didn't. We sacked everything up, and when we left out the back door, the man from the audience and a few other guys were outside waiting.

"Thankfully, there were a couple of cops out there, or we might have gotten our asses whipped. We got everything packed up in the trailer, and the cops escorted us away from the theater. They didn't let the guys who were waiting on us follow us, thank God. They had us outnumbered," Don said.

I asked Don whether it was ever confirmed that the guy in the crowd actually said something to Melba. He replied that he couldn't remember what Melba had said about it. Still, he said he was on stage the entire time she was performing and didn't hear anyone say anything inappropriate or derogatory about her. He also added that if he had heard such comments, he would have dealt with them on the spot.

Instead of leaving town, they went to the Holiday Inn a few miles away, where they had reservations. It was late when they got to their rooms, but everyone met in one of the guys' rooms to unwind from the day's events.

Don continued:

> We were in someone's room, Dickens' I think, and of course, everyone was drinking. Except Dickens. I think he popped a couple of L.A. Turnarounds (amphetamines). Things got kind of loud, so someone from the hotel came up and told us to keep it down. Well, everyone left, except me, Gary, Arnie, Jimmy, and George. George was sitting in a chair, still drinking, and Dickens was acting really hyper and talking really fast.
> Well, George looked at him and said, "You better simmer down, squirt. Or else I'm gonna stuff your ass in a suitcase and put you in the hallway."
> All of a sudden, Dickens jumped on the bed, wearing nothing but boxer shorts, a wife-beater tee shirt, and his cowboy hat. He doubled his fists up and said to George, "Come on, pal. I'll whip your ass right now."
> When he said that, George grabbed the lamp off the end table and smashed Dickens over the head with it. He knocked his ass out."

I asked Don what happened then.

"Nothing," he said. "We all went back to our rooms and left Jimmy lying on his bed. The next morning, no one said anything about it. I don't think George or Dickens even remembered it."

Chapter 14

Live at Dancetown USA

On February 11, 1965, George Jones and the Jones Boys arrived in Houston, Texas, for a three-night engagement at Dancetown USA, a popular dance hall that could accommodate over 1,000 people. Their performance was originally scheduled for two nights, but due to high ticket demand, it was extended to three.

George's manager, H.W. "Pappy" Daily, arranged for George and the Jones Boys to record a live album during their performance at the club. In the 1960s, live country albums were uncommon, and many of the few that were marketed as live recordings were actually studio sessions with canned applause added for effect.

The Jones Boys arrived a couple of hours before showtime and were greeted by a sound engineer from the Houston recording studio that would be recording their performance. According to Don, the band was aware that a live recording was planned, but they were not informed until they arrived at the club that it would take place that evening. The band set up their equipment just as they would for any other performance. The only difference was the addition of three microphones that the sound engineer brought in to capture the performance.

The album is available in three different formats: an LP released in 1985 and two CDs. The first CD, which I used as a reference while writing this book, was released in 1988. A second CD was released in 1992. There are important differences between the three releases. I'll point those out later.

The first track on the album is an instrumental piece titled "Hold On," featuring Gary on lead guitar. Interestingly, the band is about two-thirds through the song by the time the album starts.

At the end of "Hold On," a man's voice can be heard saying, "I'd like to hear 'One More Time' before George comes (unintelligible word). Please, 'One More Time.'"

Don promptly responds, "Okay. Here's 'One More Time' for Tex."

Don mentioned that a devoted fan named Tex regularly attended George's shows across Texas and Oklahoma. He always stood right in front of the stage and talked continuously during performances. Although Don couldn't remember Tex's real name, he noted that everyone simply called him Tex.

Don delivers a powerful rendition of the song, with Gary providing harmony. This is a rare live recording of the two brothers singing together on stage during this era.

Once the song concludes, Don thanks the audience and introduces George by saying, "Right now, we'd like to introduce our boss to you. A young man who records for Musicor Records. Let's all come together and give a big hand to America's number-one country singer, George Jones!"

As George steps onto the stage, the band begins playing his iconic song, "White Lightning," his first number-one hit in 1959.

After the performance, George greets the audience by welcoming them to Dancetown USA. He expresses his delight at being back, saying, "It's great to be here this time in a little better shape than when we had the flu last time."

Don mentioned that they had played at Dancetown USA multiple times and did not recall being sick during any of those occasions, although he acknowledged it was possible.

George starts to introduce his next song, but gets distracted. He invites the audience to the dance floor and encourages them to occasionally applaud the band, adding that doing so "makes us work harder." He also mentions Don and the Jones Boys before beginning the song "Something I Dreamed."

About two-thirds of the way through the song, when George sings, "So it must have been something I dreamed," someone from the audience chimes in, "I dreamed it too." I have listened to this album well over a hundred times, and that comment always makes me laugh.

As the band plays the final notes of "Something I Dreamed," the crowd erupts into applause, noticeably more vocal and enthusiastic than before. The beer is clearly flowing, and everyone is having a great time. A man in the audience shouts, "Achin' breakin' heart, George! Achin' breakin'!" referencing George's hit song from 1962, "Aching, Breaking Heart." This voice sounds similar to the one that had earlier exclaimed, "I dreamed it too," suggesting it was the same man, likely Tex.

Another man's voice can be heard requesting, "The Window Up Above." This prompts a lengthy back-and-forth between George and the crowd. George thanks the audience for their ovation amidst the ongoing applause, whooping, and hollering. He then says, "Tex, I'm going to have to ask you to hold it down a little bit," chastising Tex for being too loud and coming in over the mic. George appears slightly annoyed but does his best to keep a light-hearted tone.

Then, as if feeling a bit guilty for calling out Tex, George adds, "Here's a tune we'll play for Tex, though. He likes this one."

A woman interrupts George, saying, "Go ahead and smile."

To which George replies with perhaps the funniest line of the night: "Honey, I been tryin' to smile all night, but I don't feel that good yet. Wait'll the next session. Next time up, we'll feel better."

The crowd continues to stir, and someone, probably Tex, asks, "Are you ever going to do 'Achin' Breakin' Heart'?"

George then says, "Okay, here's 'Aching, Breaking Heart.'"

We then hear Don ask in a hushed tone, "Which key is this, B?"

George answers, "A."

The band then kicks off "Aching, Breaking Heart."

As "Aching, Breaking Heart" comes to an end, the audience erupts into enthusiastic applause. George responds by saying, "Thank you so much. You might notice that we're a little hoarse tonight, but we hope to improve as time goes on." This statement serves as his self-assessment. A vocalist of George Jones' caliber would certainly be aware if his voice wasn't at its best. However, to the average listener, including myself, his performance is outstanding. In the Paul Leslie Hour podcast interview, Gary mentioned that George had never sounded better than he did during this performance.

George continues by introducing his next song, "We Must Have Been Out of Our Minds," a Top 5 hit he recorded with Melba Montgomery in 1963. Miss Montgomery frequently appeared on package shows with George, and when she did, they almost always performed this song together. On the occasions when she was not with him, George often sang the song as a duet with Don, much to the crowd's delight. "Melba's not with me tonight, but Don Adams is, and he does a great job playing Melba," George says, provoking laughter from the audience. "We'll do our own version of it. It goes like t his."

During their performance, George and Don would change a few words in the song, which made the crowd laugh. At one point, George yelled "Whoa!" and shortly after, Don let out a loud shriek. Don explained that this routine always garnered a positive reaction from the audience. George would shout because Don playfully goosed him, while Don would jump and yell when George pinched him on the butt. This playful banter was a regular part of their act and was repeated at nearly every show during that time, especially at dance hall performances.

The next song is the popular "The Window Up Above." After finishing it, George mentions that someone has requested a fast song. "We don't usually perform rock-and-roll numbers," he says. "However, we'll give it a shot. It goes like this." Although George doesn't seem particularly excited about performing the song, Don notes that he almost always honored requests at his dance hall shows.

The band then launches into Larry Williams' song, "Bony Moronie," and Gary is on fire. Although George repeats the same verse multiple times and misses a few words, he puts his heart and soul into it. We can also hear Arnie doing things on the drums that we typically don't hear in traditional Jones numbers. The crowd responds enthusiastically.

George transitions to the next song, "She Thinks I Still Care," which reached number one in 1962. He then introduces the steel guitarist Buddy Emmons for an instrumental performance. However, George fumbles his words and appears unsure about which song Buddy will play. Eventually, he settles on, "How about 'Rio City Chimes'? That'll be a really pretty one."

Buddy then begins an upbeat instrumental called "B Bowman Hop." The Jones Boys provide excellent accompaniment, with Little Red Hayes standing out on the fiddle and Gary impressing on lead guitar. Interestingly, the album releases from 1985 and 1988 list the song as "Rio City Chimes," while the 1992 release correctly identifies it as "B Bowman Hop."

The next number is "Accidentally on Purpose," released as the B-side to "Sparkling Brown Eyes" in 1960. It reached number 16 on Billboard's country singles chart.

After singing "Accidentally on Purpose," George addresses the crowd for a few moments, during which someone repeatedly asks him to sing his "latest song." This is an unusual way to make a request. Why didn't the man simply ask for the song by name? The recording took place on February 11, 1965, and at that time, George's latest song was "Least of All," released three months earlier in November. Interestingly, George does not perform that song during the show. However, he likely sang it during the closing set, which was not recorded.

George introduces the next song, "Who Shot Sam?" This song tells the story of a shootout in New Orleans and has a vibe similar to "White Lightning." Released in 1959, it reached number 7 on Billboard's country singles chart. Don plays a significant role in the song, providing harmony and repeatedly asking, "Who shot Sam?"

After the song concludes, George tells the crowd that they are "going to take a short liquormis... er, I mean intermission." This prompts a woman from the audience to respond, "Hurry!" The band then wraps up the set with a brief instrumental piece called "C Jam Blues."

George's comment about a "liquormission" was not well received by Pappy Daily, and this was one of the reasons the performance was shelved for two decades.

After the intermission, the band comes back on stage to warm up the crowd, while George waits in the wings, possibly having another drink.

The band kicks things off with "Jonesy," a fast-paced instrumental that had become the unofficial theme song for the Jones Boys.

After performing "Jonesy," Don transitions smoothly into Ray Price's hit song, "Please Talk to My Heart." His vocals are flawless, and Gary does an excellent job providing harmony. As the band finishes the last note of the song, an inaudible announcement is made over the PA system.

Next, Don introduces the song "Sing a Sad Song," mistakenly calling it "Sing Me a Sad Song." The song was written by his childhood idol, Wynn Stewart. Although Stewart performed the song live, Merle Haggard was the first to record it in November 1963. This marked Haggard's first hit record, achieving moderate success by spending three weeks on the country singles chart, where it peaked at number 19. Stewart later recorded the song in 1976, reaching number 11. Don's live rendition of the song is impeccable, once again showcasing his impressive vocal range. Following Don, Buddy Emmons performs an instrumental piece titled "The Panhandle Rag."

Next, Don performs Buck Owens' classic song "Act Naturally." I love how Don slurs the title when introducing it, but I love his performance even more. He nails it!

After Don finishes the song, the sound of instruments being tuned and people shuffling around on stage can be heard. I can't help but wonder if Don is glancing at George, checking whether he's ready to return to the stage. At that moment, a man's voice comes over the PA system, announcing, "Joanne

Ballard, please come to the front. Joanne Ballard." I've often wondered why Joanne Ballard was called to the front and if she knew she was mentioned on the album. When Don introduces George, the band begins to play, and Little Red Hayes performs a brief flourish with his fiddle that almost acts like a reset. It's only a couple of notes, but they sound really good.

George comes onstage and begins singing an upbeat version of "I'm Ragged, But I'm Right," a song he recorded as a single in 1955. The song also appeared on his first album, *Ragged But Right*, released in 1957. Although it never charted, the song gained popularity with audiences, and George included it in his live sets for many years.

After George finishes the song, he addresses the audience, welcoming them and expressing his hope that they have a great time. The crowd begins to chatter, with most comments directed toward George. One particular comment comes from Tex, who is requesting a specific song. However, his slurred speech makes it difficult to understand what he is saying, likely because he has consumed too much beer. Someone on stage, possibly Don, responds to Tex with a sharp remark. While it's unclear exactly what he says, it might be something like, "Be quiet, Tex!" or something similar.

The next song is "Poor Man's Riches," followed by "Tender Years." Then, without hesitation, George introduces the next song as "Where Does a Little Slobbin' Tear Come From." The actual title is "Where Does a Little Tear Come From."

At that point, George introduces guest artist Rufus Thibodeaux, a fiddle player from Lake Charles, Louisiana, who performs a song called "Jole Blon."

Don mentioned that he was unsure why Thibodeaux appeared on the show. "None of us had any idea who he was," Don recalled. "He was a really nice guy. I guess George must have known him and invited him to perform a song. Between sets, George told me he was going to bring him out. That was the first time I heard about it. We never saw him again after that."

After Thibodeaux finishes his song, George returns to the microphone and says, "Very good. Little Red Hayes and Rufus Thi-b-dick", Two By Four, from Bayou Pawpaw, Louisiana." George is slurring his words and mixing them up, which leads me to conclude that he stepped off stage during Thibodeaux's performance and had a drink or two.

Next, George performs "Big Harlan Taylor," a song about a man who loses the love of his life to another man.

After the song, the crowd starts shouting requests at George, including one for him to sing "White Lightning" again. George giggles and dismissively replies with a quiet, "White Lightning," before introducing "another sad ballad." This time, he performs "She's Lonesome Again."

George finishes his song and immediately starts his closing number, "The Race Is On," released just five months earlier. This song became a chart success for George, reaching number 3 on the Billboard Country Chart in January. Additionally, it appeared at number 96 on the Billboard Pop Chart, marking a rare accomplishment for a George Jones song.

After finishing the song, George thanks the crowd and says, "We'll see you in a little bit," indicating that there would be another set. Unfortunately, that additional set was not included on the album. The Jones Boys concluded both the set and the album with the instrumental outro titled "Hold It."

There has been considerable debate over the years regarding the lineup of the Jones Boys on this recording. Some sources claim that Johnny Paycheck played bass and provided backup vocals, even though Don Adams is credited with lead vocals on seven songs. Throughout the show, George talks about and addresses Don, while Johnny is not mentioned at all. Additionally, it is often stated that Buddy Emmons filled in on steel guitar for Sonny Curtis. Some of these claims suggest that Sonny was excluded from the recording because of a lack of musicianship, but this is unfounded. The reality is that Sonny had been let go shortly before this recording to make room for Doug Jernigan to join the Jones Boys. However, Doug had not yet arrived, so Buddy Emmons was hired to step in.***[1]

Fiddle player Charlie Justice is also absent from the recording. Instead, Kenneth "Little Red" Hayes plays the fiddle. The reason for Hayes stepping in for Justice is uncertain; it is possible that Charlie was ill or took a break to be with his family, but the exact reason is unknown. Nevertheless, Don stated that it had nothing to do with Charlie's musical abilities.

---

1. *** Sonny Curtis was let go to create a position for Doug Jernigan. Doug was brought on at Gary Adams' request, but he never actually played with the Jones Boys because George fired the Adams Boys before Doug had the chance to join the band on the road. As a result, Sonny was rehired.*

For this performance, the Jones Boys on stage included: Don Adams on bass and lead vocals, Gary Adams on lead guitar and backup vocals, Arnie Adams on drums, Buddy Emmons on steel guitar, and Little Red Hayes on fiddle.

The recording's date has also been a topic of debate. Some sources suggest it was made in June 1965, while others claim it was recorded in February or March of that year. However, I am confident that the recording took place on February 11, 1965, for two key reasons.

First, there is no record of George Jones and the Jones Boys performing at Dancetown USA in the first half of 1965, except for the dates of February 11-13. Second, the Adams Boys were fired shortly after their performance at Dancetown USA, likely around February 20, and they spent most of the following months performing at various clubs across the Midwest. Therefore, they would not have been present if the recording had been made in March or June. By that time, Johnny Paycheck and Jack Watkins had joined George, but they were not featured on the album. This is evident because, once again, Don plays bass and provides backup vocals on the album, while Gary can be heard singing alongside Don in at least two songs.

The recording of this live performance sat in storage for twenty years. Pappy Daily was not satisfied with the recording, nor were the people at Musicor Records. It simply was not "clean" enough for a country album in 1965. The noise from the audience, onstage chatter, audible PA announcements, George's banter with the crowd, and his noticeable mistakes, such as forgetting song titles, announcing to the audience he was hoarse, mispronouncing Rufus Thibodeaux's name, and referencing a "liquormission" doomed the plans for a live album.

Finally, in 1985, *George Jones Live at Dancetown USA* was released on vinyl LP by Ace Records. Notably, this album did not feature any material from the Jones Boys, including Don Adams, nor did it include George and Don's rendition of "We Must Have Been Out of Our Minds" or George's song "Tender Years." The album cover depicts George Jones and the Jones Boys on stage; however, the musicians featured on the album are not the Jones Boys, who are on the recording. While the Adams brothers are shown on the cover, Sonny Curtis and Charlie Justice appear instead of Buddy Emmons and Little Red Hayes.

In 1988, the CD version that I used for reference was released. It includes material from the Jones Boys, featuring Don Adams, along with George and Don's rendition of "We Must Have Been Out of Our Minds" and George's song "Tender Years."

In 1992, a new CD titled *George Jones and the Jones Boys Live in Texas 1965* was released. This CD contains the same material as the 1988 release but uses mono audio, which some say sounds better than the earlier version. Personally, I can't discern a difference, especially since I am nearly deaf in one ear. However, this CD includes breaks between tracks, which detracts from the ability to fully immerse oneself in the music. In contrast, the 1988 CD plays continuously, providing a much better listening experience. Additionally, the album cover for this release features a 1962 photo that includes only two performers from the album: George Jones and Gary Adams.

Both CD releases come with inserts that claim to include photos and information about the recording. However, this information is highly inaccurate regarding the participants and the recording timeline. Furthermore, the inserts contain numerous contradictions, so it's best to disregard their contents.

If you decide to invest in the album, I suggest the 1988 CD version. Alternatively, it is available on YouTube.

George Jones Live at Dancetown USA is the most important live recording from the Golden Age of country music. There's nothing else quite like it. Its cultural significance is immense, and it deserves preservation. No other recording captures that magnificent time in the same way. Listening to it is almost like opening a time capsule.

Chapter 15

George Fires the Adams Boys

J ust days after recording the live album at Dancetown USA, George fired the Adams Boys, probably after their February 20 show in Jackson, TN.

Two main issues likely influenced George, particularly his manager, in the decision to fire them. First, George had missed several shows over the past few months. Many of these performances were package shows featuring other artists who relied on the Jones Boys to back them on stage, as those artists did not have their own bands. Artists such as Loretta Lynn, Melba Montgomery, Grandpa Jones, Minnie Pearl, Bill Anderson, and many others depended on their support.

The Jones Boys earned an additional $10 for each extra act they supported on the bill, in addition to their regular pay. If they backed two acts, each band member would earn an extra $20. If they backed five acts, the additional amount would increase to $50. This arrangement provided them with a great opportunity to earn extra income.

George's road manager reportedly confronted the Adams Boys and demanded that they return all or at least a portion of the extra pay they had received.

In response, Arnie replied, "That money belongs to us, and we've already sent it home to our families."

When the road manager persisted, Arnie allegedly told him, "I'll give you every dime, but you'll have to whip my ass to get it." That ended the conversation.

It doesn't make sense for George or his road manager to confront the Adams Boys about money that they rightfully earned by supporting other artists, as this was standard practice. Perhaps George made the demand in the heat of an argument, fully aware that he had no legitimate claim to the money. Arguments can sometimes turn emotional like that. Who can say for sure?

The second issue is likely the primary reason why Don, Gary, and Arnie were fired. According to Doug, Gary informed him that they were fired because, during at least one instance in January, when George missed a package show, they refused to perform for other artists unless they were paid more than the standard ten-dollar rate. When the artists denied their request, the three Adams brothers refused to go on stage, leading to the show's cancellation. That refusal may have been grounds for George's manager, "Pappy" Daily, to fire the Adams Boys.

Don told me that Sonny Curtis and Charlie Justice were also fired, but got their jobs back by "kissing George's ass" and blaming everything on Don, Gary, and Arnie.

After the Adams Boys were released, Don contacted Eugene "Pork" Marshall, the owner of the Harmony Lounge in East Moline, IL. Don asked Marshall to hire the Adams Boys to perform at his club. Since Marshall had seen them play with George a couple of times before, most recently on November 27 of the previous year, he knew that the Adams Boys would draw a crowd. Consequently, he booked them for several week-long gigs from March to May, with the first performance scheduled for March 16 to March 21.

When they arrived in East Moline, Gary called Doug to let him know that they had been fired. (Don was rehired by George in May and played off and on with him for at least the next year.)

There Ain't Nobody That Skinny

On March 25, 1966, George Jones and the Jones Boys made another appearance on the Jimmy Dean Show. This time is different from before, since Don is now the only Adams brother in the band.

After George finishes singing his opening song, "Take Me," Dean comes out to talk to him. They talk a bit, and just as Dean starts to introduce George's next song, "I'm A People," he turns to look at Don and says, "His bass man works with him on this. I'd like you folks to look at that."

George interjects, "Mockingbird legs."

Dean continues, "Ain't nobody that skinny, man. He's standing back there with them boots a while ago, and he looked like a killdee standing in two shotgun shells. His name is Don Adams. Would you believe it, Don Adams?"

The kildee reference is obviously aimed at Don's skinny legs, and the comment about his name being Don Adams is a reference to the comedian Don Adams, who was a regular guest on Dean's show.

Don smiles throughout the bit, but it's the kind of smile that makes me believe that Don wanted to punch Dean square in the face. This is another one on YouTube deserving of a peak.

PART THREE

Between the Legends

Coal Shed Publishing

Chapter 16

Enter Doug Jernigan

Gary Adams and Doug Jernigan were both talented musicians and close friends. Together, they formed an exceptional duo, with their musical collaboration lasting over a decade and their friendship enduring for a lifetime. In 1970, they recorded an album titled *Sounds of Doug Jernigan and Gary Adams*. The following year, they toured for three weeks with country artist Stonewall Jackson. From 1972 to 1976, they were members of Johnny Paycheck's band, The Lovemakers, during which time they toured and recorded together. Throughout this period, they wrote songs and performed at The Demons Den in Nashville. At one point, Gary even stayed on Doug's couch in his Nashville apartment.

In late 1964, 18-year-old Doug was staying with the Arthur Brewer family in Albany, Georgia, while he played steel guitar with a local band called the Curtis Gordon Band. When George Jones and the Jones Boys came to Albany to perform at the Shrine Temple, the Curtis Gordon Band opened the show. Other performers included Melba Montgomery and her brother, Peanut Montgomery. Doug was excited about this opportunity because he had been hearing Don's recently released single, "I Just Lost My Favorite Girl," on the radio, and he really liked it.

"I was a George Jones fan, but it was Don (Adams) that I really wanted to see," Doug recalled when I interviewed him the first time for this book. "His record, 'I Just Lost My Favorite Girl,' was getting a lot of radio play. I thought he had a great voice, very unique for the time, and I really wanted to see him perform live," said Doug.

About halfway through the opening performance by The Curtis Gordon Band, Gary came out to watch from a seat in the audience. Doug caught Gary's attention with his steel guitar playing, and Gary was impressed by the performance of the 18-year-old.

When the show ended, Gary got Doug's phone number and promised to call him soon.

In January or early February, Gary, determined to get Doug in the band, approached George with an ultimatum: "If you don't hire that kid from Florida to play steel guitar, I'm going to quit."

George, clearly not wanting to lose his talented lead guitarist, replied, "Well, you better go tell Sonny then," referring to Sonny Curtis and implying that Gary should inform him of his being let go.

Gary called Doug to share the news that he would be George Jones' new steel guitarist. However, things took an unexpected turn. Doug recalled:

> I was really excited to play for George Jones. I thought I had finally made the big time, so I packed my things and got ready to go. Then, Gary called me and said they had been fired. I was really disappointed at not getting to play for George. Well, Gary told me they were playing at a club in East Moline, Illinois, and he wanted me to join them. They had stolen two or three sets of uniforms from George, and he thought they could alter a couple for me. So, I took a bus from Albany to East Moline.

Upon arriving in East Moline, Doug thought to himself, "Here I am, playing with the Adams brothers. I've made it big." However, he was soon to receive a big dose of the Adams Boys' personality, leaving him wondering what he had gotten himself into.

Doug continued:

> When I got to the motel they were staying at, I went into the room and started setting up my old Fender 1000 (steel guitar) that I was playing then. Well, Gary and I started working on some things when Arnie Adams came over and picked up the rag I carried my bars and picks in. I wrapped them up in an old, dirty dish rag because I didn't have a bag or anything.

Arnie looked at that rag and said, "What's that here?"

I told him, "That's where I keep my picks and bar."

Then he walked over and flushed it down the commode! I went running towards him and said, "Don't flush that! That's where I keep my bars and picks."

Arnie just laughed and said, "If you're gonna hang out with us, you're gonna have to get you a bar bag and put your picks and bar in that. "Try to be cool, you know?"

So, I got me one later and put my picks and bar in it.

It is important to understand that Doug's addition to the Adams Boys Band greatly enhanced their already impressive sound. Doug and Gary developed a unique musical chemistry that complemented each other perfectly, eliminating the rivalry that often arises between a lead guitarist and a steel guitarist in bands. This collaboration marked the beginning of a partnership that would evolve over the next decade, establishing the Gary Adams-Doug Jernigan duo as a benchmark in country music.

While performing at the Harmony Lounge, the band became acquainted with a family that attended nearly every other night to enjoy their music. One evening, after a performance, the family invited the band to join them for Sunday dinner. They accepted the family's invitation, and the following Sunday, drove to their home for dinner.

"We had a real nice dinner," Doug recalled. "After we got done eating, Don, Arnie, and Gary stood up. Don said, 'Well, we don't like to eat and hang around.' So, I stood up, and we all left."

Doug laughed hard while telling me that story and went right into another one:

> It was on that same gig when Don sat down at the table one morning and got out an old Albert can and some rolling papers. I figured maybe he didn't have any packs of cigarettes, so he was just gonna roll up his own. Well, those three started smoking, and I knew by the smell that they weren't smoking cigarettes. I was only 18 years old and had grown up in the country, so I'd never smoked marijuana and didn't really know anything about it. They laughed at me, and eventually I started smoking it with 'em. So, that was my introduction to the Adams boys.

After their engagement at The Harmony Lounge, the Adams Boys Band, now featuring Doug Jernigan, packed up and headed to Milwaukee for a gig at a venue on West State Street called Nick's Nicabob. The Nicabob was a legendary country music venue owned by Nick Beaumont, known for showcasing some of the biggest stars of the day, including Jerry Lee Lewis and Patsy Cline. The decor blended Western saloon style with Victorian-era bordello aesthetics.

After setting up their equipment, Don, Arnie, and Doug enjoyed a drink, while Gary enjoyed several. By the time they started their first set, Gary was quite drunk. A large crowd had gathered, and the band sounded fantastic. However, there was one problem: Gary was feeling a bit wobbly, so he sat down on a stool while continuing to play.

After the first set, the boys took a break, and Beaumont approached Don. "I wish your brother would ease up on the drinking and stand up. It looks bad for him to be sitting down like that," Beaumont said to Don.

Don glanced over at Gary, who was still drinking, then turned to Beaumont. "I'll tell him, but I doubt it'll do any good."

As they took the stage for the second set, Don said to the rest of the band, "Boys, if I tell you to sack 'em, sack 'em up as quick as you can. We'll get everything loaded into that U-Haul trailer and get outta here."

Don's concern was two-fold. For one, there were several large bouncers on duty that night who may have been in-clined to reinforce what Beaumont had said to Don. And two, if the crowd got angry, there could be a riot.

Despite Don asking him not to, Gary sat down on his stool again to start the second set. Sure enough, after the second or third song, here came Nick Beaumont and two big bouncers towards the stage.

Don saw them coming and said, "Sack 'em, boys. It's time to go."

With that, Don Adams and the Adams Boys packed up as quickly as they could and took off for Greenfield.

When they arrived in Greenfield, Doug moved into the Adams family home on Taylor Street and became almost another member of the family. It was a crowded house with Frank and Kate, Gary, his sisters Elaine and Marcie, Marcie's husband and their two kids, and Gary's younger brothers, Farrell and Darrell.

Doug has fond memories of his stay in Greenfield, not just of music, but also of Marcie's teasing; she referred to him as a "little Rebel heathen," and of Kate's cooking. Kate introduced Doug to white gravy and egg noodles, two foods that he had never known while growing up in Florida.

Doug met Paul Angel for the first time and, over the next few months, had the chance to participate in jam sessions with Angel, the Adams Boys, and other musicians who visited the area. This experience was invaluable for both Doug and

Gary, as it helped them develop a unique sound that would distinguish them in the years to come.

The decision to return to Greenfield may have been driven more by economic factors than anything else. The rising costs of hotel rooms, meals, gasoline, and other everyday expenses associated with traveling around the country may have become overwhelming. Now that they were managing their own bookings instead of relying on George Jones' agent, their performance schedule was significantly reduced, which in turn impacted their finances.

While in Greenfield, Doug performed with the Adams brothers, primarily in weeklong gigs at The Harmony Lounge in Illinois, and on Saturday nights at the Paxton Theater in Bainbridge, Ohio.

In late August or early September, Doug received a call from his mother in Pensacola. She informed him that he had received a letter from Uncle Sam indicating that he was being drafted into the United States Army. As a result, Doug packed his gear and took a bus home. By late September, he was inducted into the Army, where he would serve for the next two years as a combat engineer, including a tour in Vietnam.

I asked Doug what his impression of the Adams brothers was after meeting them and playing music with them for a few months.

He said, "Oh man, I didn't know what to think. I had heard they were bad to fight among themselves and they were always on the verge of hooking up, but I never actually saw them fight until later. I told my dad when I got back to Pensacola that I didn't know what to make of those guys. They were very talented, but they were always on alert and ready to fight. Another thing: they were brutally honest, and if you asked them what they thought, they'd tell you, no matter how it hurt your feelings. You always knew where you stood."

Thus concluded the first chapter in the long collaboration between Doug and the Adams Boys. However, Doug Jernigan would return as things were just getting started.

Chapter 17

Merle Haggard and Michael Landon

In July 1965, Merle Haggard was on the verge of becoming a major country music star. The previous November, he had released the single "(My Friends Are Gonna Be) Strangers," which reached number 10 on Billboard's Country Music Chart. This was his third consecutive single to chart and his first to break into the top ten.

Haggard spent the first half of 1965 performing in clubs throughout California alongside his wife, Bonnie Owens, who received top billing. In June, he joined Buck Owens for a show in Albuquerque, New Mexico. (It should be noted that Bonnie Owens, Buck Owens' ex-wife, did not participate in that show.)

Merle Haggard's album, *Strangers*, was scheduled for release in September. To generate buzz for the album, Capitol Records organized performances for him at various venues across the country, including two shows in central Ohio. At that time, Haggard had not yet formed his famous band, The Strangers, so he was supported by the Adams Boys, who were already in Ohio and scheduled to perform at the same events. These performances took place on July 4 at Ponderosa Ranch and on July 5 at Frontier Ranch, both country music parks located less than three hours apart.

On July 4, Haggard, along with Bonnie Owens and the Adams Boys, performed an Independence Day show at Ponderosa Ranch, a popular country music venue in Pataskala, Ohio, near Columbus. The venue was billed as "Ohio's Most Beautiful Country Music Park." The headline act for the show was Michael Landon, best known at the time as "Little" Joe Cartwright on the television show *Bonanza* and later as Charles Ingalls on *Little House on the Prairie*. Although Landon was primarily known as an actor, he also had a music career as a teen idol type. He had recorded several songs, including a recent ballad titled "Linda Is Lonely."

Before the show began, the Adams Boys were relaxing at picnic tables in a shaded area of the park with their families, who had traveled from Greenfield to watch the performance and enjoy the fireworks scheduled for later that night. Michael Landon sent word to them, asking them to come to his dressing room to go over a few things and rehearse before the show. While this seemed like a reasonable request, Arnie and Gary disagreed. They responded by sending word back to Landon that if he wanted to rehearse, he could come outside and do it. It remains unclear whether any rehearsal actually took place, but this exchange certainly set an ominous tone for the evening.

At one point, Landon emerged from the dressing room dressed as "Little" Joe Cartwright, complete with a green corduroy jacket, beige hat, and red bandana. Several children, including Arnie's six-year-old son, Brent Adams, and his siblings, approached Landon. He was very kind to them, talking with them, signing autographs, and posing for photos.

Brent recalled a particular little boy in the crowd who seemed disheveled and less well off than most of the other kids. "Michael Landon gave that little boy his green jacket," Brent recounted during an interview with me. "He was so happy. There was a twenty-dollar bill in the pocket. I'm sure Landon knew it was there. I'll never forget that."

The Adams Boys opened the show by performing covers of several songs originally recorded by George Jones, Buck Owens, and Ray Price, along with Don's song, "I Just Lost My Favorite Girl."

Bonnie Owens followed the Adams Boys and sang several of her own songs, including "Why Don't Daddy Live Here Anymore?" and "Don't Take Advantage of Me," before introducing Merle Haggard.

Haggard's set would have included his two previous charting singles, "Sing a Sad Song" and "Sam Hill," along with his current and biggest hit to date, "(My Friends Are Gonna Be) Strangers." He and Bonnie Owens would also have performed their duet, "Just Between the Two of Us."

Michael Landon, still dressed as Little Joe and sporting a backup green jacket, took the stage to close the show. While there are no reports on how well he performed, it's safe to say the kids enjoyed his act, and many of the women did as well, given Landon's good looks. However, his singing ability fell short of that of Don Adams and Merle Haggard, which was likely noticeable to any audience members more focused on the music than on Landon's visual appeal on stage.

According to Don, Landon came off as arrogant towards the band, which caused some friction. In all fairness, the Adams Boys probably came off as a little arrogant to Landon as well. A clash of egos, perhaps.

On July 5, the same lineup performed at another outdoor music venue: Don Adams and the Adams Boys, Bonnie Owens, Merle Haggard, and Michael Landon. This event took place at Frontier Ranch in Salem, Ohio, just southwest of Youngstown.

The Frontier Ranch show was identical to the Ponderosa Park show from the day before. The order of appearance, the set list – nothing changed. Until Landon took the stage, that is.

Steel guitarist Doug Jernigan recalled that during his performance, Michael Landon felt the music was too loud. He turned to Gary in the middle of a song and said, "You're playing too loud. Turn the volume down."

Gary, refusing to let anyone dictate his volume, looked Landon in the eye and said, "Fuck you!" He didn't turn the volume down until he unplugged his amp at the end of the show.

It is safe to say that Michael Landon and the Adams Boys did not keep in touch after the shows.

I asked Don about his impressions of Merle Haggard and what Haggard thought of the Adams Boys.

"I knew he was going to become a star. He was a great singer and a great entertainer. People really liked him. He was also impressed with us; he told me that he really enjoyed playing with our group. We all got along very well, and I suppose we just connected on a musical level," said Don.

They would meet again further down the road.

Chapter 18

Little Jimmy Dickens TV Tour

On September 7, 1965, Little Jimmy Dickens released a single on Columbia Records that would become the biggest hit of his career: "May the Bird of Paradise Fly Up Your Nose." This novelty song, notable for its unusually long title, features three verses, each depicting a scenario in which a miserly man rudely insults another person, including a beggar, a laundryman, and a cab driver.

On November 20, "May the Bird of Paradise Fly Up Your Nose" reached number one on the Billboard Country Chart, where it remained for two weeks. The song spent a total of 18 weeks on the country chart and peaked at number 15 on the Billboard Hot 100 on October 16. This marked Dickens' only appearance on the Hot 100.

Columbia Records aimed to capitalize on the song's success and boost record sales by booking Dickens to perform it on several popular television shows. Dickens was tasked with putting together a solid band to accompany him, so he reached out to his old friend, steel guitarist Buddy Emmons. Emmons signed on and, knowing they were available, recommended the Adams Boys. Dickens eagerly hired them. To say that Buddy Emmons and the Adams Boys constituted a solid band was a massive understatement.

According to Don, in October, Dickens was interviewed by Ralph Emery of WSM Radio during Nashville's annual DJ Convention. They discussed Dickens' latest hit record and his upcoming television tour to promote it. The interview went something like this: At one point, Emery said, "Jimmy, let's talk about your band. I understand you will be accompanied by Buddy Emmons and the notorious Adams Boys."

Dickens answered, "That's right. I've known Buddy for a long time and he's just a fine fine steel guitar player. I've got to know the Adams brothers too. We've played a lot of the same shows over the last few years when they were with George Jones."

Dickens paused for a second and added with a chuckle, "Touring with the Adams Boys is just like riding with the James Gang."

Don believed that exchange marked the first time the Adams Boys were publicly referred to as "notorious." The label stuck.

The first stop on the television tour was New York, where a taping of the musical variety series *Hullabaloo* took place. The show aired on Monday evenings from 7:30 PM to 8:00 PM on NBC. It was broadcast on November 8, although the exact taping date is unclear; it likely occurred sometime between November 3 and November 5. The episode was hosted by The Serendipity Singers, a popular folk group. Guests included Marvin Gaye, Dusty Springfield, and Donovan, in addition to Dickens. It was quite an impressive lineup.

Dickens and his band performed on a raised stage constructed from rough lumber designed to evoke a country feel, while the Hullabaloo Dancers performed a high-kicking hokey dance in front of the stage, wearing costumes with a stereotypical country-western flair.

Most performances on *Hullabaloo* were lip-synced because the producers thought it provided a more polished sound for television. However, for reasons unknown, it was decided to have Dickens perform live.

Dickens was struggling to keep time during the taping, and after several flubbed takes, the decision was made to have him lip-sync the song while the band pretended to play. Still, he was having trouble keeping time, and the producers were concerned that the taping was taking too long and that production costs would exceed the show's modest budget. Someone had the idea to have Arnie, known for his impeccable timing and sitting directly behind Dickens, play drums along with the record to help him stay in time. The idea worked, and the performance was wrapped up in just one take.

I asked Don why Dickens was having so much trouble keeping time. After all, he was a seasoned performer and had performed thousands of shows in his career. "He was just terrible at it. He couldn't keep time. He was either too fast or too slow, and he never knew when to come in. It could be exhausting at times playing with him," Don said.

A black-and-white video of the performance is available on the *Getty Images* website. In the video, when the camera zooms in on Dickens, both Arnie and Gary are clearly visible, delivering convincing performances. Gary, in particular, appears to be enjoying himself, grinning widely in response to the humorous lyrics of the song.

On November 20, the same day that "May the Bird of Paradise Fly Up Your Nose" reached number one on the charts, Dickens appeared in Nashville as a guest on *The Bobby Lord Show*. Unlike previous performances, Dickens did not bring his band; instead, he performed with Bobby Lord's house band, which was customary for guests on the show.

On November 26, Dickens and the band were in Miami Beach, FL, for a live performance on *The Jimmy Dean Show*. George Jones was also on the show, leading to a reunion of sorts between him and the Adams Boys. Backstage, Don and George were talking when Dickens joined them. George asked Dickens if Don could sing tenor for him that night. Dickens, perhaps remembering when George smashed a lamp over his head in Buffalo, replied, "Hell no! Use your own damn band, Jones."

A video of the performance is available on YouTube.

On November 27, the band traveled from Miami to New York for a live appearance on *The Tonight Show Starring Johnny Carson*, which was scheduled for November 29. This meant they would be in New York for three days with little to keep them occupied. Such situations often led to trouble for anyone associated with the Adams Boys, and this trip to New York would be no exception.

Don said that Dickens brought a briefcase filled with amphetamines on the trip and consumed them rather liberally.

> The morning after we got to New York, Jimmy called us all into his room. He threw that briefcase down on the bed and opened it up. It was clear full of amphetamines—speed. He had a big grin on his face and said, "Get you some breakfast, boys."
> I told him, I didn't want any of that shit. Those pills just weren't our thing. I mean, we all had one every now and then. Everyone in Nashville did. Gary did it more than me and Arnie did. I think he had a couple that morning, but I'm not sure. He probably did. When you took those things, you'd be up for two or three days. I didn't like that.

The next morning, before breakfast, Dickens entered the room shared by Arnie and Don. According to Don, Dickens was being "especially ornery" that day. "It wasn't anything specific," Don recalled. "He was always a bit hyperactive, but that morning he was really wound up. He just kept talking and bouncing around, which got on our nerves. Eventually, Arnie had had enough. He grabbed hold of Jimmy and stuffed him in the closet. Then he propped a chair under the doorknob to lock him in. Jimmy yelled and pounded on the door, but we just left for breakfast. We returned about two hours later and let him out. Arnie told him to 'behave yourself or back in you go!' Jimmy didn't say a word."

Apparently, the four-foot-eleven-inch Dickens was a good sport and didn't get too upset, even when he was the target. "There was no point in getting mad. He was too little to do anything about it anyway," Don explained.

The show was filmed in Studio 6-B at NBC Studios, located in Rockefeller Plaza, Manhattan. Other guests that night included comedian Alan King and World Heavyweight Boxing Champion Muhammad Ali.

A humorous story involving Arnie is said to have occurred during the filming of this show. Many people believe it happened then, while others claim it took place at a Las Vegas show. However, I could not find any records of George Jones performing in Las Vegas between late 1963 and early 1965, when Arnie was in the band. Therefore, I am attributing the story to this appearance on Carson's show.

Towards the end of Alan King's stand-up comedy performance, Dickens and the band came out and took their positions in preparation for their own performance. Seeing them come out, King turned to the band and asked for a drumroll in anticipation of delivering a punchline to a joke. Everyone looked at Arnie, the drummer, but he did not respond.

King repeated his request, stating, "Drummer, give me a drumroll." Once again, Arnie did not respond.

At this point, King looked directly at Arnie and began to speak. However, Arnie interrupted him, saying, "I work for Jimmy Dickens, not you. If you ask me again for a drumroll, I'm going to knock your head off."

King, visibly surprised, turned back to the audience, finished his routine, and exited the stage.

Over the years, Don explained, when sharing the story, that Arnie didn't perform a drumroll because he didn't know how.

After their performance, Dickens and the band went backstage. There, they had the opportunity to chat with Muhammad Ali. After shaking hands, Gary turned to Don and Arnie and said, "We just shook the hand that shook the world!"

Unfortunately, Don did not mention how their performance went, and, sadly, no known surviving recording of the show is available.

After returning to their hotel, the entire group chose to go out for drinks. Dickens preferred walking a few steps ahead of the others, believing it helped disguise his short stature. This was the situation as they walked from their hotel to a bar, a couple of blocks away. Dickens led the way while the rest of the band followed behind him in a single file. Don recalled:

> It was pretty comical. Jimmy was walking out front like a mother duck, and we were all following behind him in single file, dressed in our purple suits. He was strutting along, barking orders about doing this and going there, and blah blah blah... Finally, Gary said, "I've listened to enough of his shit."

So Gary speeds up and catches up with Jimmy. Then he grabbed him and threw him on the ground. Jimmy was yelling and hollering. Gary sat on him and took Dickens' boots off his feet, then tossed them in the middle of the street. Two or three cars ran over them. We were all laughing, and Jimmy just walked out in the street in his socks and got his boots. People in cars were honking horns and cussing at him. He just pulled his boots on, and we all had a good laugh. We just fell back in line and continued walking to the bar like nothing happened.

In December, Dickens and the band traveled to Los Angeles to record performances for three afternoon dance shows: *The Lloyd Thaxton Show*, *Hollywood a Go Go*, and *9th Street West*. The recordings took place on December 12 and 13, with the broadcasts scheduled for later dates.

The Lloyd Thaxton Show, which was the most popular dance show on television during its run, recorded its episode on December 12 and aired on December 30. As was common for the show, the performances were lip-synced. This was the only one of the three shows in which the band was featured on air with Dickens. Unfortunately, no known video footage from this episode has survived.

On the morning of December 13, they taped *9th Street West*, and in the afternoon, they recorded *Hollywood a Go Go*, both in the same studio. The performances were to be lip-synced, and unbeknownst to Dickens, the band would not be accompanying him on stage.

While recording *9th Street West*, Dickens once again struggled to keep time with the music, and once again, Arnie came to the rescue. This time, the band sat at tables on the dance floor, directly in front of Dickens but out of view of the cameras. Arnie kept time by tapping on the table with his drumsticks, which helped Dickens complete the performance. Unfortunately, no recording of this performance is known to exist. The exact airdate of this episode of *9th Street West* is unknown, but it likely aired in January 1966.

After finishing their work on *9th Street West*, Arnie and Dickens had a disagreement as they walked to their car. The argument focused on Dickens' chronic inability to keep time, and things became heated when Dickens blamed Arnie for it. Offended, Arnie snatched Dickens' cowboy hat off his head, threw it to the ground, jumped into the air, and stomped on it several times with both feet. This time, there was no laughter; Dickens' hat was destroyed, and he was not amused.

Hollywood a Go Go was filmed that afternoon, following the same format as *9th Street West*. There are a couple of interesting details from that taping. First, a drummer, who is not Arnie, can be seen playing with Dickens. He is tucked away in the background and is hardly noticeable, but he is definitely present. This drummer helped Dickens keep time, just as Arnie did on *Hullabaloo* and *9th Street West*. In addition to performing "May the Bird Of Paradise Fly Up Your Nose," Dickens also sang "I Got Honky Tonk Troubles." Videos of him performing both songs are available on YouTube. While it cannot be confirmed that he performed both songs on *9th Street West*, there is a strong likelihood that he did. This episode of *Hollywood a Go Go* was broadcast on January 15, 1966.

The collaboration between the Adams Boys and Little Jimmy Dickens ended after the tapings in Los Angeles. However, their separation was only temporary; they would cross paths again very soon.

Chapter 19

Merle Haggard Comes to Greenfield

Merle Haggard and Bonnie Owens arrived in Greenfield on February 24, 1966, and booked a room at The Lanes Motel on West Jefferson Street. Haggard was in town because he was headlining a show at the Paxton Theater in nearby Bainbridge on February 26.

The Adams Boys Band would be backing Haggard during his performance, so they all got together at Paul Angel's house on February 25 to practice. Don described it as more of a jam session than a practice.

A packed house gathered at the Paxton Theater to watch Haggard perform. His song, "(My Friends Are Gonna Be) Strangers," had burned up the charts just a few months before, and he was well on his way to becoming one of the most popular country music artists in America.

The highlight of the show, at least as far as the Adams family was concerned, was when Haggard called the Adams Boys' youngest brother, Darrell Adams, on stage to perform one of his (Haggard's) songs, saying, "He sings it better than I do." Darrell was unaware that Haggard was going to call him on stage; by all accounts, he took full advantage of the opportunity and knocked the song out of the ballpark. Unfortunately, no one I spoke with about it, including Darrell, his twin brother, Farrell, his older brother, Don, or his friend, Ralph May, could remember which song he sang. Regardless, it was the first time that Darrell had ever been introduced on stage in front of a live audience. It wouldn't be the last time, though, as Darrell went on to entertain audiences all over the country with his incredible voice for many years.

After the show, Haggard stayed in Greenfield for several more days. It's not clear if that was the plan all along or if he decided to stick around on impulse. What is clear is that Haggard and Bonnie Owens checked out of the Lanes Motel and relocated to a guest room at the home of the Adams Boys' parents, Frank and Kate Adams, located on Taylor Street in the Higginsville section of Greenfield.

Don mentioned that he and the Adams Boys performed with Haggard at a couple of clubs in Columbus shortly after the appearance at The Paint Valley Jamboree. However, he could not recall the names of the venues, and I couldn't find any newspaper records to verify the shows. I wonder if these Columbus performances were arranged at the last minute through connections the Adams Boys had, rather than booked through the usual channels. This possibility suggests a genuine bond between Haggard and the Adams Boys.

I came across two social media accounts from individuals who claim to have attended a concert at the Pan Theater in New Boston, OH. The show reportedly featured Merle

Haggard, Bonnie Owens, and the Adams Boys, and both accounts state that it took place during the early part of 1966. However, I have been unable to find any records to verify these claims.

While staying with the Adams family, Haggard recorded a demo of a song at Paul Angel's house, where Angel had set up a recording studio in the basement. The song, titled "I'm a Lonesome Fugitive," was given to him by Nashville songwriter Liz Adams, who had also written his hit single "(My Friends Are Gonna Be) Strangers." Angel provided Haggard with the original recording and kept a copy for himself. Haggard later recorded "I'm a Lonesome Fugitive" for his 1967 album of the same name, and it became his first number-one hit, launching him to superstardom.

Frank and Kate Adams left a lasting impression on Haggard during his brief stay in Greenfield. Frank was an accomplished fiddle player, and Haggard enjoyed listening to him play. In the evenings, he joined Frank and the rest of the Adams family for impromptu jam sessions in their living room. Many years later, Haggard told Don that Frank was among the inspirations for his song "Daddy Frank (The Guitar Man)," which reached number one in 1971, marking Haggard's tenth number-one hit.

As for Kate, it was her country cooking that impressed Haggard the most. Don mentioned that whenever he encountered Haggard in the years that followed, he would often say, "Don, I'd give anything to go back to Greenfield and have a big old bowl of your momma's beans and cornbread."

A couple of nights before Merle Haggard and Bonnie Owens were set to leave Greenfield for California, Haggard approached Don and Arnie with a proposition. "I'm about to start a tour up and down the West Coast," Haggard said. "I would like you guys to come with me and be my band."

Intrigued by the offer, Arnie asked, "What's the pay?"

"I can pay you twenty dollars a show," Merle answered.

Arnie and Don exchanged glances, and then Don asked, "How many shows do you have booked?"

"Right now? One," Haggard said.

Don smiled and said, "I think we should stay here for now."

At that time, it was entirely understandable for the Adams Boys to decline Haggard's offer. Don and Arnie had families to support and were working steadily, headlining the Paint Valley Jamboree in Bainbridge and making regular appearances at the bars around Greenfield. Leaving to pursue a music career on the West Coast was a risky endeavor, more suited for single men than for those with families.

Looking back, the decision to stay in Greenfield could have altered the course of country music history and deprived the Adams Boys of their greatest chance for enduring success in the genre. Just a few months later, Haggard formed his band, The Strangers, and the rest is history.

Chapter 20

The Roger Miller Incident

In 1965, a talented young singer from Montana signed a recording contract with RCA Records. While this might not seem particularly noteworthy at first glance, it becomes significant when we consider that the singer was Black. At that time, there were very few Black country singers, and none had achieved stardom. However, this was about to change.

On December 28, 1965, Charley Pride, hailing from Helena, Montana, released a record titled "The Snakes Crawl at Night." To promote this new release, a short tour of Montana was organized for late April 1966. The purpose of the tour was to help prepare Pride for his upcoming trip to Nashville and a planned tour of the United Kingdom in May.

Pride was scheduled to be part of a package show that also featured Johnny Paycheck and The Cashiers, Carl Bellew, Johnny Darrell, and Karen Kelly. The Cashiers consisted of the Adams brothers, Don, Gary, and Arnie, along with steel guitar player Jimmy Crawford. They would serve as the opening act and provide backing for each performer, as they were the only band on the tour.

Don, Gary, Arnie, Johnny, and Jimmy Crawford left Greenfield in Don's car for a long drive to Glasgow, Montana, towing a U-Haul trailer that Johnny rented, loaded with their equipment.

The tour was split into two segments, each comprising three weekend shows, with two evening performances per show. The first segment included stops in Glasgow on April 22, Great Falls on April 23, and Helena, Pride's hometown, on April 24. The second segment featured shows in Kalispell on April 28, Missoula on April 29, and Anaconda on April 30. There were no performances scheduled from April 25 to 27, giving the musicians a few days off to relax.

The first segment went smoothly, with ticket sales for all three shows doing well, including a sold-out performance in Helena, Pride's hometown.

During the three-day break, things took an interesting turn when country star Roger Miller unexpectedly showed up at the hotel where Don and his group were staying. Don was unsure about the reason for Miller's visit. Although I couldn't find any records of Miller performing in Montana at that time, it's possible he actually was. It's also possible that he was there on vacation or perhaps wanted to see Charley Pride perform. No one knows for sure. Regardless, Roger Miller was at their hotel in Montana during the break, and by April 28, the day of the show in Kalispell, both Miller and Johnny Paycheck had left.

Johnny missed the show in Kalispell, leaving the promoter furious. Pride's manager, Jack Clement, reached out to his booking agent, Jack Johnson, in Nashville to find out where Johnny had gone. Clement informed Johnson that the last time anyone had seen Johnny, he was with Roger Miller; both of them were very drunk.

Johnson contacted an associate of Miller and discovered that Johnny had traveled to California with him.

According to Don, when Johnson inquired about why Johnny left the tour in Montana to head to California, Johnny explained, "The Adams brothers stole my car and trailer and drove back to Ohio. The trailer had all of my equipment and uniforms in it." It's important to clarify that the car belonged to Don, and the Adams brothers were still in Montana at that time.

"Years later, Johnny told us that he had gone to California to play steel guitar for Roger Miller," Don recalled. "They had been drinking and just went to the airport and got a flight to L.A. John said he didn't even remember flying out there; he just woke up the next morning in California."

Johnny missed the entire second segment of the tour, leaving The Cashiers in a difficult situation. Since Johnny left before being paid, the band members did not get paid either, aside from the money they earned for backing up the other performers.

After the tour ended, Don and the boys loaded everything up and headed back to Greenfield. When they arrived, Don parked the U-Haul trailer in his parents' yard on Taylor Street. It stayed there for two or three years until someone stole it. It's unknown whether or not Johnny ever paid for it.

A couple of days after returning to Greenfield, Gary received a call from Johnny. Johnny was scheduled to perform at The Bayfront in St. Petersburg, Florida, on May 8, alongside the sultry icon Jayne Mansfield. He was playing with a band his manager put together called the Little Darlings, but the lead guitarist couldn't make it to the show. So Johnny asked Gary to come to St. Petersburg to perform with him.

Gary said he would, but only on one condition: Johnny would have to wire him $40 in advance before he would agree to come. Adjusted for inflation, that would be over $400 in 2026. This was a steep fee for a guitarist to perform at a single show in 1966.

Johnny protested and offered Gary less money, but Gary remained firm, reminding Johnny of the incident in Montana just a week earlier when they didn't get paid. Eventually, Johnny agreed and wired the money to him.

The show, titled *Jayne Mansfield and the Country Music Spectacular*, also featured Sonny James, Hank Snow, Jim Nesbit, and Tommy Cash.

Miss Mansfield made three appearances on stage, totaling about ten minutes.

Gary and his cousin, Red Dog, drove to St. Petersburg for the show and returned to Greenfield the following day. This would be the last time that any of the Adams Boys would perform on stage with Johnny Paycheck for five and a half years.

Chapter 21

Standing in for the Buckaroos

The Adams Boys had performed at numerous country music shows over the years, but they had never purchased a ticket to watch as fans in the audience. That changed one day in March 1967, when Don, Gary, and Arnie climbed into Arnie's car and drove from Greenfield to Cincinnati to see Buck Owens and The Buckaroos perform at Music Hall.

Arriving about an hour early, the three brothers went backstage to greet their old friend, Buck Owens. Owens welcomed them warmly, and as they reminisced, someone brought an urgent message telling him that his band, The Buckaroos, could not make it to the show because their bus had broken down north of Indianapolis. With less than an hour until showtime and a capacity crowd of over 3,500 fans eagerly waiting, this posed a serious problem.

Owens contemplated the situation for a moment and devised the only solution he could think of, besides canceling the show: he asked the Adams Boys to join him on stage.

It's important to remember that Don, Gary, and Arnie were present as fans. They didn't have their instruments with them and had no intention of performing on stage. However, recognizing the tough situation their old friend was facing, they agreed to help, provided they could find instruments to play.

Other artists on the lineup included singer Jim Ed Brown and singer/comedian Don Bowman. Both were dependent on The Buckaroos for musical support, as they only had their own guitars. For this show, though, they would be on their own.

When Gary asked to borrow Bowman's guitar and amplifier, Bowman readily agreed. This left Don and Arnie needing a bass and a drum set. The best Arnie could manage was a pair of drumsticks he found lying on the back seat of his car and a hatbox that had previously contained Owens' hat. Meanwhile, Don was unable to secure a bass, and he was worried about what to do with his hands on stage. He rummaged backstage and found an old tambourine and briefly considered taking it onstage. However, he ultimately decided against it, later saying, "Slapping a tambourine on my leg would have been too humiliating."

When it was time for him to go on, Owens addressed the audience to explain the situation and introduced his impromptu band for the evening. He referred to them as "The rhythm section that made George Jones a star." While this wasn't entirely accurate, it certainly had a nice ring to it.

The performance exceeded expectations. Owens sang all of his hits, and Gary delivered a stellar set, as usual. Arnie kept impeccable time on Owens' hatbox, while Don's backup vocals were perfectly on point. Throughout it all, Don casually hooked his thumbs in his front pockets.

Looking back, Don said, "The crowd appreciated our effort and cheered for us. I was a mess, though. It was the only time in my life that I felt nervous on stage. I thought I was going to throw up. I was so anxious that my pant leg was shaking. But, I felt fine once we started playing."

Everyone in the audience that night received a free ticket to what was promised to be a makeup show later in the year. While most people gratefully accepted the ticket, I doubt that the makeup show was nearly as memorable as this one.

Chapter 22

Going Their Separate Ways

The late 1960s are hard to document. The three brothers largely went their separate ways and did their own thing throughout much of this period.

Don and Ferlin Husky

Don was concentrating on solo appearances and also did about an eight-month stint with Ferlin Husky. He told me that Ferlin Husky was probably the only person in country music he couldn't stand to be on stage with:

> I hated every second that I was on the road with Ferlin Husky. His music was not my style. And he had a habit of starting songs either too fast or too slow, then trying to change the tempo halfway through the song. He always ended up turning

around and saying something smart to the band,
like it was our fault.

About the second or third time he did that to me,
I told him, "Oh no, you're the one who started out
the song too fast, so you'd better be able to sing
it that way. You turn around one more time and
embarrass the band in front of the crowd, and I'll
knock your ass off this stage."

After about eight months, Don couldn't take it anymore.
He just went home.

Arnie and Eddie at Carnegie Hall

In 1966, Arnie and the Adams Boys' first cousin, Eddie Adams,
who had just graduated from high school, got a job working
with Little Jimmy Dickens.

According to Eddie's son, Randy Adams, Little Jimmy Dick-
ens and his band, including Arnie and Eddie, were in New
York playing a package show with Buck Owens and others at
Carnegie Hall.

When it came time to leave the hotel for Carnegie Hall,
everyone piled on Owens' bus for the ride there. Apparently,
everyone except Eddie got on the bus before it departed, and
no one realized it.

Eddie came out of the hotel just as the bus pulled off
and gave chase, boots in hand, trying to catch it or get its
attention so it would stop.

A young lady on the bus noticed Eddie running after them
and said, "That poor fan has been chasing this bus for several
blocks."

Arnie looked out the window at the man she was referring
to and said, "Wait a minute. Stop the bus. That's not a fan.
That's Eddie. Driver, stop and let Eddie on the bus!"

When Eddie got on the bus, he collapsed from near exhaustion, but by all accounts he recovered and put on a heck of a show.

A few months later, Eddie was drafted into the Army, and his singing career was put on hold. Later, he adopted the stage name Grizz Sawbuck and dressed in buckskins, creating a mountain man image. I couldn't determine how long Arnie stayed with Dickens after Eddie left, or whether he did at all.

Throwdown in Omaha

There occurred an incident sometime around 1968 that has become a legend in the story of the Adams Boys. The Adams Boys Band, which at the time consisted of Don, Gary, Arnie, and Darrell Adams, along with Doug Jernigan, who had been discharged from the army, was playing a two-week gig in Omaha, Nebraska. Their accommodations while in Omaha consisted of a nice apartment built under what used to be a bowling alley.

Towards the end of the gig, on day ten or eleven perhaps, Gary had a little too much to drink before the show, leading him to play jazz behind Don instead of playing the song straight, as Don expected.

Don chastised Gary on stage for doing so, which led to an argument after the show. The two continued to argue in the car on the way back to their apartment, and they nearly came to blows when they got out of the car before going inside. Once inside, the two stood chest to chest with one another, ready to fight. At that point, Arnie stepped in between them, saying, "Listen, you two, you're not going to destroy this place. If you want to fight, take it outside."

At that, Don picked up an iron from an ironing board and hit Arnie in the shoulder with it. Arnie retaliated by punching

Don in the mouth, knocking out, depending on who's telling the story, two, three, or even four of Don's front teeth. At that, Gary jumped on Arnie, knocking him to the ground. Don then tried to pull Gary off of Arnie, and Arnie grabbed hold of Don, pinning him to the ground while Gary ran off.

Darrell and Doug were watching all this happen when Don looked up at Darrell and said, "What the hell, Darrell? Aren't you going to do something?"

When I interviewed Darrell at his home in Nashville about this incident, he told me that he had no intention of intervening because there was no way on earth he was going to fight Big Arnie.

Doug mentioned, when I interviewed him about it, that there was blood everywhere, but Gary and Don stopped fighting almost as quickly as they started, hugged one another, and started laughing.

Don was unable to sing without his front teeth, so Darrell, who had been sharing vocals with Don, took over as the lead vocalist for the rest of the gig while Don just played bass.

When they got back to Greenfield, Don got false teeth to replace the ones that Arnie knocked out, and according to Darrell, it improved his smile immensely.

Gary and Doug on the Road

Gary and Doug Jernigan played for five or six months with Little Jimmy Dickens in 1968 and about three weeks with Stonewall Jackson in late 1970 or early 1971.

I'm not 100% sure why they left Dickens, but at least one funny story came out of their time on the road with him. Gary and Doug got kind of loud in their hotel room one evening just after midnight. Little Jimmy, who was staying in a room next to them, came and knocked on their door. Doug opened the door, and there stood Little Jimmy Dickens, wearing only his boxer shorts, T-shirt, and Stetson hat. Dickens looked at Doug and said, "Listen, pal, you're going to have to hold it down in here because I need to get some sleep."

At that point, Gary came to the door, looked Dickens in the eye, and removed the Stetson from his head. He took a bite out of the brim, then placed it back on Dickens' head. Dickens didn't say a word. He simply turned and walked back to his room. But when paychecks came out a couple of days later, Gary had a large deduction to pay for a new Stetson.

A couple of years later, Gary and Doug got a job playing with Stonewall Jackson. They went out with him on a three-week tour, and while on tour they were tasked with selling merchandise: t-shirts, posters, pictures, and the like.

When the tour ended, Stonewall paid Gary and Doug for their labor but only gave them a small percentage of the merchandise sales. Gary and Doug asked for a larger cut. Stonewall refused, so they quit.

Solo Records and Side Projects

Jack O' Diamonds

In 1967, Don signed a new record deal with Jack O' Diamonds Records and went right to work, recording four songs slated for release as singles. The songs were "Why I Still Love You", "Brand New Bed of Roses", "Two Of the Usual", and "Just Say You Love Me." The four songs were likely all recorded at the same session.

All of the records received airplay, but, like D Records and even Musicor to an extent, Jack O' Diamonds did not invest heavily in distribution to record stores, focusing more on garnering radio airplay than on record sales. Despite that, "Two Of the Usual" went to number 64 on the Billboard Country Charts, marking Don's first appearance on the charts. A significant achievement!

Bridge Over Troubled Waters

In late 1969 or early 1970, the Adams Boys fully embraced their Christian faith and set out on the road, performing at churches across the eastern half of the country. Sometimes they performed by themselves, but more often than not they traveled with evangelist and former country singer Dave Rich and his ministry, planting new churches in underserved areas. The band at this point consisted of Don, Gary, and Arnie, as well as their brother Darrell and sister, Marcie, on vocals, and cousin Joe Adams on steel guitar.

In 1971, they recorded and independently released a gospel album titled *Bridge Over Troubled Waters*. The album was recorded at Rusty York Studios in Cincinnati.

Don, Darrell, Marcie, and their brother Farrell share vocals, with Darrell singing lead on six of the 12 songs. *Bridge Over Troubled Waters* stands as a fine example of the Adams family's musical talent, especially Darrell's vocal skill.

The album was reissued on CD in 2005.

Sounds of Doug Jernigan and Gary Adams

In January 1972, Gary Adams and Doug Jernigan released an instrumental album that, at least in my estimation, turned out to be a true hidden gem, combining three music styles: Country, Jazz, and Soul. The album is called *Sounds of Doug Jernigan and Gary Adams*. Gary plays guitar on the album, of course, and Doug plays steel guitar. The other session musicians were bassist Larry Randolph, drummer Billy Brow, and pianist, oboist, and flutist John "Yogi" Cowan-

The album, produced by Jon Buskirk, was recorded in late 1971 at Rome Recording Studio in Columbus, OH, and released on Starr Records. The director was Don Hales. I'm not sure what an album director does, but I assume Hales was actually a co-producer. Regardless, he is listed as "director."

The album contains eight tracks. The first tune on side 1 is an instrumental called "T.K.O." written in the studio by Gary and Doug. Doug told me that Gary wrote 90% of it. It's a great number that they went on to play frequently at Johnny Paycheck shows between 1972 and 1976.

Also on side 1 is a medley of songs, "Dixie," "Battle Hymn of the Republic," "Hey Jude," and "Fire & Rain," arranged by Doug and Gary. What stands out on this nearly 8-minute track is Gary's vocals on "Fire & Rain." I describe Gary's performance as "haunting." Not as in a frightening spiritual haunting, but the haunting one feels when they conjure up the melancholy of their past. A kind of longing, if you will. Just an incredibly moving performance.

Sounds of Doug Jernigan and Gary Adams can be found on eBay and occasionally in used record stores. If you can find it, buy it!

According to Doug, he and Gary recorded a second album a few years later, but they were unhappy with the sound, and it was never released.

The Boys

Three years later, in 1975, the Lovemakers, calling themselves The Greenfield Express, recorded a double LP titled *The Boys*. The album contained 24 songs and was recorded at Rome Recording Studios in Columbus, released on Rome Records. I'm sorry to say I haven't listened to the album, but I can't imagine it being anything but good.

Chapter 24

The Demons Den

In late 1969 or early 1970, Doug Jernigan moved to Nashville, while Gary spent time in the city but did not make a permanent move there.

Together, they regularly performed at various venues throughout town, sharing the stage with notable artists such as Buddy Emmons, Don Rich, and Jimmy Day. They frequently played shows at the Demon's Den, a club located on Broadway Avenue.

One evening at the Demons Den, a young man carrying a guitar case approached Gary and asked to join him and Doug on stage for a jam session. Initially, Gary brushed him off, but the young man persisted, returning night after night with the same request.

During one of my many interviews with Doug for this book, he shared the following story: "There was a guy who kept begging Gary to let him come on stage and jam with us. At first, Gary kind of ignored him, but eventually, I guess he got tired of the guy asking. Finally, Gary said to the guy, 'Are you as good as me and Doug?' The guy responded, 'Of course not. I'm not as good as you two.' Gary then replied, 'Well, then you can't get up here and play with us.' That was how Gary was. Very particular about who he allowed on stage with him, and if he didn't think you were good enough, he would let yo u know."

Ralph Sees Stars

In mid-October 1971, Don had a late-night show scheduled at the Demons Den in Nashville during the annual DJ Convention, which took place from October 14 to October 17. The backing band for Don's performance included none other than Gary Adams on lead guitar, Buddy Emmons on bass, and Doug Jernigan on steel guitar. The identity of the drummer remains unclear.

Ernie Stepp drove Don to Nashville for the show in his black 1970 Cadillac Eldorado. Tagging along were Ralph May and Steve Marple, both making their first trip to Nashville.

On April 12, 2025, I interviewed Don and Ralph at Don's home in Greenfield. We had a three-hour conversation that was incredibly valuable, entertaining, and funny. In short, it was pure gold. Much of the information used in this book came from that interview. Ralph remembered:

> I had just come back from basic training and was living in an apartment in Greenfield. They (Don, Ernie, and Steve Marple) pulled up outside and honked the horn, so I went out, and Don said, "Come on, we're going to Nashville."
> So, I said, "Okay, let's do that."
> That was my first trip to Nashville. This was before the interstates were finished. So, we went

through all these little towns in Kentucky, and Ernie wanted to drive right through the middle of town and run every stoplight.

I told Marple, "We're going to get pulled over somewhere." Because he was running every stoplight in these little towns. We were in a hurry because Don was supposed to be there by midnight, and we were cutting it close. So Ernie was laying on the gas all the way. He wasn't slowing down for anything. We finally pulled over somewhere just outside Nashville, and Don ran in and put his stage outfit on.

Thanks to Ernie, they arrived at the Demons Den on time, and all four men walked inside.

Ralph continued, "When we walked in, Don headed towards the back but stopped and started talking to this good-looking blonde at the bar. So, I walked over that way, and it was Dolly Parton. I knew who she was, of course. She was all over television. I got to smiling because she was calling him 'Donnie.'"

According to Ralph, the place was packed. "It was DJ Convention week, and there was stuff going on all over town. You could hardly move inside, so me and Marple went outside to smoke a cigarette. Well, here comes a stretch limousine, a white one. It pulled right up to the front door, and out jumps Buck Owens and Don Rich. I recognized them, of course, and there was another guy with them that I didn't recognize."

After finishing their cigarettes, Ralph and Steve went back inside. Ralph said:

We hadn't found a place to sit yet. The band was taking a break at a big, long table that was set up for them. Don was sitting there with Buck Owens,

Don Rich, and that other guy that I didn't recognize. So, me and Steve got a couple chairs and sat right up next to the table, as close as we could get. Everybody is talking, laughing, and carrying on. So, I got over close to Don and asked him in his ear who that guy with Buck Owens was.
Don said, "That's the guy from Creedence Clearwater Revival. John Fogerty."
I couldn't believe it! John Fogerty? My God, he was as big as the Beatles.

When the band returned to the stage, Gary informed Ralph that he would call him up to sing Ray Price's hit song, "For the Good Times," before Don came on to perform.

As the band made their way on stage, Roy Clark passed and said, "Hey, Gary!"

"Yeah! How's it going, Roy?" Gary said.

"I just wanted to know have you heard my new album," Clark said, referring to his latest release, *The Incredible Roy Clark*.

Gary said, "Yeah, my sister, Marcie, bought it for me. I played it once and took it back."

Clark busted out laughing. "You didn't really do that, did you?"

"Yeah, I did!"

Everybody had a good laugh.

"Gary would do things like that," Ralph said.

Don interjected, "He (Gary) was brutally honest. Key word 'brutally.' If you wasn't any good at something, and you thought you were, he'd be happy to bring you down." Then Ralph said:

I remember one time we were in Cincinnati, someplace listening to this band. And Gary was talking to the steel player. The guy told Gary that he just had two more pedals put on his steel and a bunch of other stuff. Gary looked at him and said, "Well, if you could just learn to play it, you'll be alright."

We went over to the Sunnyside (a small bar near Hillsboro, OH) one time to listen to a band. They wanted Gary to come up and sit in on a couple songs. So Gary did, and later, when they were taking a break, Gary was talking to the singer, a guy we knew named Sam. Gary asked him, "How long you been playing with these guys?"

Sam says, "Oh, about six months. They're my friends."

Gary looked at him and said, "You need to find some new friends." And they heard him, too! Gary didn't care.

Thinking again of that night in Nashville, Ralph said he was in awe. Not only did he get up on stage and sing, he witnessed a big crowd, including some of music's biggest names, Dolly Parton, Buck Owens, Don Rich, John Fogerty, and Roy Clark, sitting at tables listening to a band made up of guys who were, or soon would be, legends in their own right: Gary Adams, Don Adams, Buddy Emmons, and Doug Jernigan.

If anyone needs a real-world example of the respect that the Adams Boys had among fellow Nashville professionals, this is it. The stars sitting in that audience as fans speak louder than anything.

Chapter 25

Road Life

I love road trips and try to avoid interstates whenever possible to explore the backroads, especially U.S. Routes and state roads that wind through the heart of America. Instead of taking bypasses, I enjoy driving right through the centers of cities and towns, from Abingdon, VA, to The Bronx, NY; from Knockemstiff, OH, to St. Louis, MO; and from Columbia, TN, to Dallas, TX. If you want to experience America as it truly is, take the backroads.

Michelle and I take several road trips each year. Sometimes our trips last a couple of days, while other times they extend to a couple of weeks. Our greatest adventure was a two-week drive along U.S. Route 1, from Fort Kent, ME, to Key West, FL. It was an incredible experience, showcasing a diverse cross-section of Americana. In hindsight, we should have taken three weeks.

It's my love for backroad travel that sparked my interest in stories that focus on the everyday lives of Don, Gary, Arnie, and their bandmates as they traveled from show to show throughout the 1960s and 1970s.

When I was with Don, we mostly talked about big performances and funny incidents, but I always made sure to dig deeper to set the scene for the stories. I wanted to enhance the narrative, or garnish the plate, so to speak. I was curious about the big show in Houston, but I also wanted to know what they had for breakfast, how they received their mail, where they did their laundry, and what conversations unfolded as the miles rolled by, day after day. Initially, Don didn't understand my interest in those mundane details. However, I explained to him that what he considered "just life" was incredibly fascinating to those of us who had never experienced it.

I have documented 293 shows that the Adams Boys played with George Jones between May 1962 and May 1966. Honestly, that might be as little as one-third of the number of shows they actually performed, as records are incomplete. You must also remember that they quit or were fired a few times along the way, or they would have played even more. Still, that translates into thousands upon thousands of miles traveling between shows.

In the 1970s, while traveling with Johnny Paycheck, I documented 273 shows from August 1972 to October 1976. Once again, these records are incomplete, meaning that this number represents only a fraction of the actual performances.

These totals do not include the miles they traveled on their own over four decades, nor do they account for the miles they traveled with Johnny when he was known as Donny Young. Additionally, the totals do not include the miles logged with Paul Wayne, Ray Price, Merle Haggard, Little Jimmy Dickens, Ferlin Husky, Stonewall Jackson, Barbara Fairchild, or Marty Robbins.

We're talking a couple of hundred thousand miles.

It's the early to mid-1960s; four, five, or sometimes even six guys were traveling all over the country, sometimes in a bus, but more often than not in a Cadillac DeVille or Eldorado, or a Lincoln Continental, or even a Dodge Polara. Big roomy beasts with V8 engines, averaging 9 to 14 miles per gallon of gas, or less when you consider the trailer they almost always hauled behind them.

The guys took turns driving, with Don and Arnie doing the most because they enjoyed it. Don mentioned that fiddle player Charlie Justice also drove frequently after joining the band.

Gary also drove, but according to Don, he didn't have much stamina late at night or early in the morning. On several occasions, while everyone else was sleeping, Gary would get sleepy, and instead of waking someone else to take over driving, he would simply pull the car over, close his eyes, and go to sleep. A couple of hours later, one of the others would wake up to find the car stopped, causing them to arrive late for shows or barely make it on time. One time, after pulling off to the side of the road to sleep somewhere in Arizona, Gary threw the car keys into the desert after Arnie smacked him in the head for not waking anyone up. It took over an hour to find the keys.

Once, Arnie was driving through San Francisco on his way to a show when he got pulled over for speeding. When the police officer asked for his driver's license, Arnie couldn't find it, so he was arrested and taken to jail. Meanwhile, the rest of the band continued on to the show and performed without a drummer for that night and a few subsequent shows. A couple of days later, one of them found Arnie's driver's license, and they stopped to bail him out of jail on their way back through San Francisco.

One thing that occurred to me is how a car hauling around a half dozen grown men for weeks at a time must smell. So I asked Don.

"I'm sure you can imagine," he said, with a grin. "Everyone smoked cigarettes then. Farting, belching. Why do guys think it's so funny to make other people smell their farts?"

I couldn't stop laughing at that moment.

Don continued. "Smelly feet too. And not everyone showered like they should."

"Does anyone come to mind for not showering frequently enough?" I asked.

"Gary," he said. "Gary needed reminding sometimes. George (Jones), too."

It's worth noting that I have never met anyone as conscious of his appearance as Don Adams. He enjoyed looking good both on stage and off. He mentioned that this trait came from his father and once told me, "I won't even go to the store what I don't wet my hair first."

The conversation led to further questions about hygiene and cleanliness. I learned that while backing George, the Jones Boys typically traveled with three stage uniforms. Don explained that they usually wore each uniform twice before moving on to the next one. However, this rule was not strict, as they also needed to match George's outfit. According to Don, over the years, they had uniforms in a variety of colors, including purple (his personal favorite), blue, gray, black, and green, among others. Regarding cleaning, Don mentioned that most towns they visited had at least one dry cleaning service that would pick up uniforms in the morning and return them within six to eight hours.

George provided the band members' uniforms, while they usually brought their own boots. However, there was at least one occasion when George bought boots for everyone. For instance, he purchased a pair of black boots adorned with white lightning bolts on the sides. Gary was very fond of those boots and wore them often, but Don and Arnie found them too small, so they rarely wore them.

Everyone made sure to get a fresh haircut before starting a new tour. If they needed a trim along the way, they either visited a local barber or did it themselves. Dry shaving was a common practice, especially if they went directly from one show to another without checking into a hotel.

Don emphasized to me on several occasions that the teasing between him, Arnie, Gary, and their bandmates was severe. Especially in the 1960s when they were younger.

"The teasing and joking was brutal," said Don. "Me, Gary, and Arnie were the worst, but Buddy (Emmons) was almost as bad. And so was Glen Davis. Someone was always getting pissed off."

Don continued, "My cousin, Red Dog, was on the road with us for a while. He worked for George as a sort of valet. He'd run errands for him, get his clothes cleaned, bring him whiskey to drink, things like that. One time, me, Gary, Arnie, and Buddy got on him so bad that he got off the bus and quit. Red Dog used to smart something off, then look at Buddy and nod and smile. He liked it when Buddy laughed and joined him in attacking someone else. Well, we were down south somewhere, and he said something smart about one of us and looked at Buddy and smiled. This time, though, Buddy rolled his eyes, looked over at us, and nodded and smiled. So we all rolled our eyes, nodded back to Buddy, and pointed at Red Dog. He got mad, so we all let him have it then. It was rough. He just got off and went back to Ohio."

I asked Don if Red Dog was a frequent target for their abuse.

"No more than anyone else. He (Red Dog) usually gave it right back and would attack anyone at any time. He just had enough that day, I guess. I probably didn't see Red Dog for three or four years after that. George hated losing him," said Don.

Don added another humorous story about the joking and teasing. "We were in Nashville, getting ready to head out to Texas to do a round of package shows with Hank Cochran (another popular singer of the day) and some others for a few weeks. George had told Hank how brutal we were with the teasing, and Hank wanted to see for himself. He told George that he'd ride the bus with us and get us under control. George had already told us that Hank said that he would straighten us out on the bus. Anyway, as soon as the bus pulled out, we got started. Hank tried to shame us and tell us that we shouldn't joke around like that. Well, me, Gary, and Arnie started on him and gave it to him bad. George and his wife were traveling together in their car and were ahead of us. A hundred miles down the road, we pulled over for gas, and Hank got off the bus and got in with them. He told George, 'Those guys are crazy as hell. I couldn't take that shit anymore.'"

As for hotels, Don said that he preferred to stay at a Holiday Inn whenever possible. When asked why, he said there was almost always one in the bigger towns, and they usually had a decent restaurant and an affordable bar. Sometimes they had a swimming pool as a bonus.I was surprised to learn from Don that they shared rooms to cut expenses. Sometimes they would double up in multiple rooms, and other times they would all be in one room.

"If we could get a room with two beds, Gary and Arnie might share a bed, me and Sonny (Curtis) would share one, and when we added Charlie (Justice) he would sleep in a roll away bed. If the rooms only had one bed, we'd get two rooms. We never thought anything about it. George always had his own room," said Don.

When they weren't dining at Holiday Inn restaurants or those at other hotels, the guys tended to frequent roadside hamburger and chicken stands for convenience.

George had access to a bus only occasionally throughout the mid-60s, and when he did, it wasn't always top-notch.

One of George's buses had no heat, and it would get very cold inside during the winter months, forcing the guys to sometimes take unconventional measures to stay warm.

Don said:

> The bus didn't have heat, and you would just about freeze sometimes. George was drinking a lot of Crown Royal (Canadian whisky) at the time, and we used the bags it came in (Crown Royal bottles come in purple velvet bags) to keep our feet warm. We'd stick those bags right over our feet. It didn't help much, but it was better than nothing.
> There were two occasions when George, drunk of course, pulled a gun on that same bus and may have shot someone if not for others intervening.

> We were riding along one time somewhere out west, and George was really drunk. All of a sudden, he pulls this revolver out and starts looking at everyone with a mean look on his face. I saw him looking around, and when he looked at me, I said, "George, if you point that gun at me or anyone else, I'm going to beat the shit out of you. Put it a

way."
And he did. He put it away and went to sleep. When he woke up, he didn't even know he had done it. When I told him, he felt bad about it and apologized.

The second time he pulled a gun was late one night when we were driving in a rainstorm. The driver was having a hard time seeing, so he pulled over to wait on the rain to slow down a little so he could see to drive. I guess that pissed George off because he said something like, "Get this damn bus moving."
Then there was a loud "KABOOM!"
We thought we had been hit by lightning. But it was really George's gun going off. He had put a bullet right through the floor of the bus at his feet. It's a wonder it didn't blow his foot off. Arnie snatched the gun away from him, unloaded it, and threw the bullets out the window. I took the box of bullets from him and threw them out, too.

The next morning, George apologized to everyone. He had tears in his eyes. He really meant it. He wasn't mean unless he was drunk. But when he got drunk, he was unpredictable. I kept his gun for a couple of weeks and gave it back to him when we got back to Nashville. I never saw him with a gun after that. I know other people have told stories about him pulling guns and shooting later. But I never saw it happen again after that.

Most of the members of the Jones Boys, who performed from 1962 to 1966, were between 19 and 28 years old. George was a bit older, having turned 33 in 1964. Given this age range, it's understandable that some of their antics might lead someone to say, "Now you know why women live longer than men."

For example, during the summer of 1962, as they were wrapping up a tour, George decided to buy a moped. The exact location of this purchase is unclear. In his book I Lived To Tell It All, George mentions that it happened in either Illinois or Iowa. However, in a television interview in the late 1990s, Johnny stated that it took place in Maryland. Additionally, in an interview for this book, Don revealed that Gary told him it was in Minnesota. Despite these discrepancies in the accounts, there is a reliable consensus that George did indeed purchase a moped.

After buying the moped, George realized there was no room for it on the bus. As a result, he compelled Gary and Donny Young to take turns riding the moped back to Nashville. The condition of the moped and its riders upon their arrival in Nashville remains unknown.

For entertainment, the car's radio was the main source. They typically listened to country music stations, often hearing the same songs they sang each night at shows. Don mentioned that this made it easy to sing along, adding, "At least you could hear a different DJ announcing the records as you went from city to city."

Along with enjoying country music, they spent their time listening to ball games and news broadcasts, with Cincinnati Reds games being particularly popular.

Don recalled that while driving to a show in New Mexico, he heard on the radio that President John F. Kennedy had been shot and killed by Lee Harvey Oswald in Dallas. Two days later, while in a hotel room somewhere in Texas, he watched live on television as Jack Ruby shot and killed Oswald.

Books, magazines, and newspapers were popular forms of entertainment. Paperback novels were often read aloud and shared among friends until their covers fell off. According to Don, Arnie had a particular interest in true crime magazines. There's even a photo of Arnie sitting at a table, smoking a pipe, with a true crime magazine beside him. In the days before 24-hour cable news and the internet, newspapers were in high demand.

Playboy magazine was particularly popular among the guys, and there was always a copy available. Don recounted a funny backstage story involving a copy of Playboy.

In 1964, they were performing at a package show in a large auditorium somewhere in the northeastern United States. The lineup included George Jones and the Jones Boys, Buck Owens and the Buckaroos, Minnie Pearl, and Grandpa Jones.

Before the show began, steel guitarist Sonny Curtis crossed the street to a newsstand, where he bought a newspaper and a copy of Playboy, which he carried in a paper bag.

Returning to the auditorium, Sonny settled down to read his newspaper, keeping his magazine concealed in the sack and out of sight of others.

Gary approached Sonny and leaned over his shoulder to read something in the newspaper. While doing so, he noticed the paper sack with the edge of the magazine sticking out. Curious, Gary picked up the sack, and before Sonny could stop him, he pulled out the magazine and held it up for everyone to see.

"My, Gawd!" Gary exclaimed. "What do we have here?"

Sonny hurried to grab the magazine, but Gary turned away and said with faux indignation, "Who brought this trash in here?"

Everyone in the backstage area gathered to see what the commotion was about. Poor Sonny was mortified, especially because there were at least three or four women in the group, including Minnie Pearl.

Gary opened the magazine to the centerfold while strutting around and continuing his performance of shock and disgust. Buck Owens' sideman, Don Rich, joined Gary in berating Sonny by throwing his arms in the air and exclaiming, "Shame! Shame! Shame!"

As Minnie Pearl approached, she placed her hands on her hips and tilted her head to get a better look at the buxom young woman in the centerfold photo. With a huge smile, she exclaimed, "Gary, that girl looks like she's done drunk all the milk on the farm!"

That declaration from Minnie defused the situation, and everyone had a good laugh and went back to whatever they were doing before Gary got everyone excited. Don couldn't remember whether Sonny reclaimed his magazine.

I asked Don about staying in touch with his family back home. He said that calling home was expensive, so he usually only called about once a week. However, he said that he wrote letters nearly every day. The majority to his wife, Helen, but also to his parents.

Although the guys could easily mail letters home from the hotels or by simply dropping them in any mailbox along the way, receiving mail was a little more complicated. Because they were always on the move, mail from home was sent to an address in Nashville and delivered once or twice a week by George's road manager. Don mentioned how nice it was when the mail was delivered and he received 2 or 3 letters. He described it as being "like Christmas." He said it was crushing, though, if he didn't receive any mail, which happened on occasion.

Like many musicians traveling across the country, the Adams Boys and their bandmates had their share of vices.

Alcohol was readily available throughout the country, but the locations where it could be purchased varied. In some states, alcohol was only sold in state-operated stores, while in others, it could be bought at grocery stores.

The dance halls and honky-tonks where they frequently performed all sold alcohol, whether it was only beer or both beer and hard liquor. Additionally, the hotels they stayed in typically featured a bar or restaurant that served alcohol.

According to Don, while they occasionally consumed alcohol, it was not a daily habit by any means. They typically drank after hours and away from the stage. Additionally, Don emphasized that he and the other band members never drank and drove. He also mentioned that during breaks in a performance, they preferred to drink coffee. The same didn't apply to George.

In the 1960s, marijuana was often sold in metal Prince Albert cans, typically in quarter-ounce or half-ounce quantities, with prices ranging from $10 to $20. These cans filled with marijuana were commonly referred to as "lids." So, when someone purchased a lid, they were essentially buying a Prince Albert can filled with marijuana.

Don made several references to buying lids of marijuana. He recalled that the first one he ever purchased was in San Antonio, Texas. He mentioned that he, along with Gary and Buddy Emmons, smoked the entire lid at once because they were afraid of getting caught with it. This practice became a sort of norm for them. Don noted that they didn't smoke marijuana very often, but when they did, they smoked all they had.

Amphetamines were the most widely used and easily obtainable recreational drugs during the early to mid-1960s. Doctors frequently prescribed medications like Benzedrine (commonly referred to as "Bennies"), Dexedrine (known as "Dexies"), and Drinamyl (also called "Purple Hearts") for various reasons, including treating fatigue, aiding weight loss, and alleviating depression. Additionally, it was relatively simple to request "samples" directly from pharmaceutical companies.

According to Don, nearly everyone he knew in the music business during the 1960s was openly using amphetamines. "They were everywhere," he remarked.

I once read a quote that stated, "We took three or four days to tune up, and then we jammed for a week without sleeping." While this quote may be apocryphal, it effectively highlights the widespread use of amphetamines during that period.

By the 1970s, some aspects of life on the road had changed, while others remained the same.

For the most part, they continued to share rooms, although by this time, it was uncommon for them to share beds.

Johnny Paycheck had a tour bus for the entire duration of the Adams Boys' collaboration with him from 1972 to 1976, except for a few months toward the end of 1976, when they traveled in a van with bean bags to sleep on. Unlike George, Johnny often chose to ride on the bus with the band and sometimes took the wheel.

During this time, Johnny remained sober from 1971 until early 1976, using only nicotine and caffeine. Although he was drug-free, some of the others occasionally experimented with substances. Don, Gary, and Dave Gray considered themselves to be among those who indulged, while steel guitar player Doug Jernigan did not partake at all, having given it up a few years prior. The habits of the remaining members fell somewhere in between these two extremes.

I found an almost unbelievable story in the December 11, 1974, edition of the *Greenfield Daily Times*. Johnny's tour bus broke down while they were on the way to a show near the Georgia-Florida state line. As they waited for a mechanic to arrive for repairs, a car pulled over to offer assistance. It turned out to be "Fast" Eddie Montgomery, a Greenfield resident who happened to be driving by and noticed the Paycheck bus on the side of the road. With showtime approaching, Montgomery gave the band a ride to the venue.

This story was verified by Don and others. Don stated that Johnny promised to pay Montgomery $100 for his time, fuel, and inconvenience, but he never did.

In the summer of 1975, they were at a hotel in Topeka, Kansas, eating breakfast before leaving for their next show. As they boarded the bus, Don looked around and noticed that Gary was missing.

"Where's Gary?" Don asked drummer Steve Marple.

"I don't know," Steve answered. "I haven't seen him since last night."

Don looked around the hotel but couldn't find Gary. He walked back out to the bus to see if Gary had gotten aboard, but he was not there.

"Has anyone seen Gary?" Don asked again.

Still, no one had seen him.

"What are you gonna do?" Steve asked.

Don thought for a second and said, "Fuck him. We're leaving!"

With that, Don got behind the wheel and headed down the highway without their lead guitar player.

After traveling a few miles, they heard a car horn honk. It was Gary driving a convertible with a woman in the passenger seat. Gary was sporting a big afro hairstyle that was whipping in the wind.

Don nearly drove off the road with laughter and exclaimed, "Is that Gary?"

"I think it's Carlos Santana," said Steve, pointing to Gary's large afro.

Don pulled over, and Gary got on the bus, grinning from ear to ear. When Gary saw Steve, he let out a sound that was almost like a confused, "What the hell is going on?" It came out as a drawn-out "HuuuuUUHH?" which sent everyone into fits of hysterical laughter.

Once everyone had settled down, Gary revealed that the woman he was with was a hairdresser, and she had given him the perm in exchange for the very expensive watch he had been wearing. This admission sparked another round of laughter, keeping the bus at the side of the road for several more minutes before they finally sped off down the highway. There is no indication that Gary continued to wear an afro once it finally relaxed.

In mid 1975, Johnny, on the verge of bankruptcy, made some changes to cut expenses, including giving up his own hotel room. Instead, he began sharing a room with Don.

Don told me that the time he and Johnny spent rooming together was the best period of his life on the road.

"Me and John became really good friends again after going through a period where we became more like business associates," said Don.

I asked him to explain what he meant. "It was like we never talked about home or good times from the past. We never just sat around drinking coffee and shooting the shit. Then, when we started rooming together, that changed. We started to talk about the good times we had and how far we had come. We laughed a lot. It was different, though, because we were laughing together. Not at each other."

Don went on to describe a talent that very few people knew Johnny had:

> John could imitate almost anyone. He could do Gabby Hayes better than Gabby Hayes. He had the beard, and he'd push his hat up in front. He looked and sounded just like him. And cartoon characters. Daffy Duck, Bugs Bunny, Popeye. He could do them all. When we were in Vegas in '75, we would watch cartoons on Saturday mornings, and he would imitate them all. He did a perfect Foghorn Leghorn. Porky Pig. (Don laughs) I tried to get him to do them on stage, but he never would. He could tell a joke too. Better than anyone. He could tell a joke better than anyone I ever knew. The fans would have loved it, but he never would do it. I wish he would have.

Don brought up one constant concern that he and many other traveling musicians had to contend with. Wives searching for signs of infidelity, drug use, or other evil deeds when they got home. Don said, "Every time I came off the road, Helen went over my clothes, my bags, everything, looking for phone numbers on scraps of paper, makeup on shirts, pills, anything that could get me in tr ouble."

"Did she ever find anything?" I asked.

Don answered, "Not usually. I may have slipped up once or twice. One time when we were with George, someone gave Arnie a big green jar full of pills. Speed. Arnie knocked the jar over at some point and the pills went all over the floor and in the seat. We thought we got them all picked up. But Helen went out the morning after we got home and started going through the car looking for shit. She found about a dozen pills laying around. Green ones and white ones. She was pissed off. I just told her George left them there."

A final thought on road life. I asked Don on two different occasions how he felt when a tour ended and they were headed home. He always gave me the same answer.

"It was the best feeling in the world. I always got excited during those last few days of a tour. The anticipation of getting home and living a normal life for a week or so was unbelievable," he said.

Conversely, I asked him what it felt like to get on the bus for another tour, knowing he wouldn't be home again for several weeks.

"Sometimes I thought I would rather have my arm chopped off than go back out again. It was really hard to leave the kids. But it was my job. So, I went."

PART FOUR

Johnny Paycheck

Coal Shed Publishing

Chapter 26

Legacy

“We owe a legacy to Johnny Paycheck, and had it not been for him, there would have been no Adams Boys. He picked us up when some of them didn't even want us seated next to them. Johnny Paycheck was the best friend the Adams Boys ever had.”

Don Adams

August 3, 2025

Chapter 27

She's All I Got

O n October 9, 1971, Johnny Paycheck released a song that would lift him from relative obscurity and propel him to headliner status within country music. The song was "She's All I Got," the title song to his 1971 album of the same name. It was written by Gary U.S. Bonds and Jerry Williams Jr., aka "Swamp Dog."

Freddie North released the song earlier in 1971, and it reached number 39 on the Billboard Hot 100 Chart and number 10 on the Soul Singles Chart.

Johnny's recording of the song quickly rose up the Billboard Country Chart, peaking at number 2. It also landed on the Billboard Hot 100 Chart, where it reached number 91.

Record producer Billy Sherrill heard North's version of the song on the radio and believed right away it could be a country hit. Years later, Don shared that Sherrill had told him he had in mind two artists to pitch the song to: Johnny Paycheck and Don Adams. However, Sherrill ultimately chose

Johnny Paycheck because it was widely known in Nashville that Johnny was living in Denver, CO at the time, while no one knew how to reach Don. When I asked Don how he felt about possibly recording the song if Sherrill had been able to contact him, he stated that the song wasn't a good fit for him and that Johnny was the right choice. Johnny recorded the song on August 4, 1971, at Studio B in the Columbia Recording Studio in Nashville.

Because of the song's success, Johnny put together a band, The Cashiers, and hit the road, playing shows all over the country, including a December 13 show in Greenfield at The Rand Theater. The show was a benefit for Toys For Tots, with all proceeds going toward buying Christmas presents for needy children in the Greenfield school district.

For the Greenfield show, Johnny brought along his bass player and harmony singer, Joe Diamond. However, his backing band was Don Adams and the Adams Boys Band, consisting of Don on bass and vocals, Gary on lead guitar, Arnie on drums, and Doug Jernigan, billed by the local newspaper as "Doug Journeyman" on steel guitar.

I'm not certain, but I believe this may have been Arnie's last performance as a drummer. If not, it was certainly his last BIG performance. Arnie had pretty much quit playing music by that time and was employed as a prison guard.

There were two shows: the first at 7:00 PM and the second at 9:00 PM. Tickets were priced at $2.00 for adults and $1.00 for children. The show opened with Donnie Bowsher, followed by Don Adams and the Adams Boys Band, and finally Johnny Paycheck. Don switched from playing bass to rhythm guitar when Johnny came on stage, while Joe Diamond took over on bass. It's unclear whether Don provided any backup vocals; if he did, it would likely have been singing third-part harmony on some songs, as Diamond was the main harmony singer. Photos from the early part of the first performance show a near-capacity crowd.

I have two important thoughts regarding this show in Greenfield. First, in the midst of a major nationwide tour, Johnny took time to return to his hometown and perform a benefit concert. He didn't have to do that, but he did. That poor kid from Higginsville gave back to his community, even though he could have just ignored it. Secondly, he didn't have to use the Adams Boys Band as his backup band. He had a band, and they could have performed. But he chose the Adams Boys. I know it was a benefit concert, meaning he didn't get paid. So, you could say, he did it to cut out the expense of paying his band. And while that could be true, the probability that his band would have played the show if Johnny asked them to is pretty high. At the end of the day, Johnny Paycheck shared his stage with a group of guys he grew up with instead of the band he was touring the country with. Thus giving the Adams boys an opportunity to take their careers to the next level. Mention that the next time someone is running Johnny Paycheck into the dirt.

The Adams Boys wrapped up the year with at least two local performances. While I'm unsure of the exact date, Gary and Paul Angel, along with pianist Alice Stewart, entertained at Greenfield Manor's annual employee Christmas dinner. Greenfield Manor was a local nursing home. On New Year's Eve, the Adams Boys performed at the Mini Bar, located north of Greenfield.

In the new year, the Adams Boys would have the opportunity to perform on larger stages.

Chapter 28

Riding with Paycheck

Johnny Paycheck played two shows at the Ohio State Fair in 1972, the first one on August 28 and the second one on August 29. Don and Gary traveled to Columbus on August 28 for the show and met with Johnny either before or after the show. During the meeting, one of the Adams brothers inquired about Johnny's band, The Cashiers, asking how he put them together. Johnny answered, "Oh, they're friends of mine from Denver." To which Gary responded, "You need to get some new friends." Implying that Johnny's band wasn't very good.

Johnny must have agreed because, according to the September 1 edition of the *Greenfield Daily Times*, Gary was hired to play guitar on the spot. In the September 8 edition of the same publication, it was reported that Don was hired to play bass and sing tenor, while Larry "Red Dog" Adams was hired to drive Johnny's new limousine. Steel guitar player Doug Jernigan was also hired around the same time as Gary and Don. The only remaining members from the original Cashiers were fiddle player Paul Justice and drummer Lonnie Nantz.

Around the same time, Johnny hired Ernie Stepp, as his bodyguard. Ernie was well adapted to the role. Described by some as a "gangster from Dayton," Ernie was a bona fide tough guy who spent a lot of time in Greenfield.

Don couldn't remember how they met, but told me that Ernie approached him once with a scheme to pass counterfeit twenty-dollar bills at county fairs in the Greenfield area. The plan was for Don to use the bills to make small purchases and get real cash back in change. Don would keep a portion of the change, and Ernie would get the rest. Don declined the offer, and Ernie couldn't understand why ANYONE would pass on such an opportunity.

Ernie would go on to be a very capable bodyguard for John and seemed to enjoy his job.

Based on the hire dates, I suspect that Gary's first show was on August 31 in Marshfield, WI, at the Central Missouri State Fair. Don's first show was probably on September 10 at the Mississippi State Penitentiary in Parchman, MS, for the Parchman Rodeo.

Notable shows through the end of the year were October 23 in Greenfield at the McClain High School Auditorium for the annual Toys for Tots benefit show, October 26 at Gilley's in Pasadena, TX, and December 9 in Fort Worth, TX, at the famous Panther Hall Ballroom.

On September 24, Johnny appeared solo to sing the national anthem at the Atlanta Falcons-Buffalo Bills football game in Atlanta. He sang off-key and butchered the lyrics, singing, "*O say can you see. It's cloudy at night. Those broad stripes and red bars through the perilous night.*" In all fairness, it's a tough song to sing.

In addition, there was a show on November 25 in Vancouver, BC, at the Queen Elizabeth Theatre, which was absolutely panned by music critic Jeani Read in the November 27 edition of *The Province.* Ms. Read wrote: "Johnny Paycheck's group, The Cashiers, made for only a passable after intermission warm up to Sonny James, deftly marching through Paycheck's collection of unremarkable songs under his unremarkable voice."

It should be noted that Johnny was there as part of a package show along with Sonny James, Tom T. Hall, and Barbara Mandrell. All but Hall were similarly lambasted by Ms. Read.

Between shows with Johnny, Gary managed to squeeze in two solo performances on October 14 and November 18 at the Paint Valley Jamboree in Bainbridge.

Johnny ended 1972 by following "She's All I Got" with a string of hits, including "Someone to Give My Love To," "Love Is A Good Thing", and "Somebody Loves Me." So, optimism was running high for him and the band going into 1973.

On April 18, they performed at Philharmonic Hall in New York before boarding a plane to the United Kingdom. There, they were scheduled to appear at the Fifth International Festival of Country Music, which took place on April 21 and 22 at Empire Pool (now known as Wembley Arena) in Wembley. This festival was the UK's premier country music event, and Johnny was nominated for the Top Male Vocalist award, which was ultimately given to George Hamilton IV.

Johnny performed on both days of the festival, drawing huge crowds of 9,000 fans.

On May 16, they performed at the Grand Ole Opry House in Nashville, on a show broadcast via closed circuit on HBO.

It was around this time that Gary acquired his nickname, "The Black." According to Don, he and Gary were driving in downtown Cincinnati in Gary's brand-new black Lincoln

Continental Mark IV. They stopped at a traffic light, and another car, identical except for its color, pulled up alongside them. Gary and Don already had their windows down when the driver of the other car, a Black gentleman, lowered his window, glanced at Gary over his sunglasses, and said calmly, "Nice ride, Black."

Gary thanked the man, and as the light turned green, he looked at Don and said, "Black? Uh – THE Black." Just like that, a new legend was born.

Gary Adams "The Black" Circa 1977 Courtesy of Gary Adams Jr.
"Little Gary"

Gary changed his image to match his new nickname, "The Black," frequently dressing in dark clothing, complete with a hat and boots. Some said he resembled Zorro.

This is a good opportunity to talk about Gary's penchant for what he called "guitar slinging."

Guitar slinging was when Gary got dressed up in his black outfit, went to a club where he heard a hot young guitar player might be playing, and sat in the audience waiting to be recognized by the band on stage. He knew that once he was recognized, they would ask him to come on stage and join them for a song or two.

Gary would oblige, and once on stage, put on a performance designed to thoroughly embarrass the band's guitar player. It was Gary's way of letting everyone in attendance know that he was, indeed, the best.

According to Steve Marple, Gary did this a hundred times. At least.

For the record, I once asked Steve how good Gary was compared to guitar players like Chet Atkins, Roy Clark, Sonny James, and others. Steve looked at me and said, "Eric, Gary would eat them for lunch."

On June 9, Johnny's newest single, "Mr. Lovemaker," was released and immediately climbed the Billboard Country Chart, ultimately reaching number 2. Johnny changed the name of his band from The Cashiers to The Lovemakers to coincide with the release of the song. Curiously, though, they played a show on July 24 at the Stallion Nightclub in Oxnard, CA, where they were billed as "Johnny Paycheck and The Paymasters."

The highlight of the year was undoubtedly the release of Don's album, *On His Way*, in August on Atlantic Records. It was recorded at Quadrafonic Studios in Nashville and produced by David Paul Briggs. Earlier in the year, Don had signed with Atlantic Records' new Country Music Division, alongside Willie Nelson.

The producers spared no expense and hired a stellar group of Nashville musicians to appear on the album. Among them were guitarists Gary "Showhog" Adams *** and Harold Bradley, steel guitarist Doug Jernigan, fiddle players, Paul

"Peanut" Justice, Roy Justice, and Vassar Clements, and back-up vocal groups, The Jordanaires and the Nashville Edition.[1]

Two songs from the album appeared on the Billboard Country Chart. The album's first single, "I'll Be Satisfied," peaked at number 91, while the follow-up single, "I've Already Stayed Too Long," reached number 34. This made it his highest-charting record and the only one to enter the Top 40.

Don didn't like the title or the cover of the album. He mentioned that no one had asked for his input on the name. As for the album cover, he wasn't fond of the photo featured on the front. The image shows Don sitting on the hood of a Rolls-Royce in front of a theater, with "Don Adams On His Way" displayed on the marquee. Additionally, he was bothered by the visible crease at the bottom of his right pant leg. "My pants were too short, so they let the hem out to make them longer. I wish they had cropped that damn crease out," he remarked.

During one of my many visits to see him in Greenfield, Don gave me a sealed copy of the album. I struggled with whether to remove the cellophane wrap to play it or leave it sealed. "What good is a record if you can't listen to it?" he asked. He was right. I took off the cellophane and he autographed the album cover for me, writing, "Thanks to my good friend & author." – Don Adams. I've played it a hundred times and never skip a single song.

On August 24, around the same time Don's album was released, Johnny and the band appeared on the popular music show, *The Midnight Special*. Hosting the show were Marty Robbins and Loretta Lynn. Other guests included George Jones, Tammy Wynette, Conway Twitty, Charlie Rich, Tanya

---

1. Show Hog was a self-imposed nickname that Gary humorously added to the credits of this album.

Tucker, Johnny Rodriguez, Tom T. Hall, Don Gibson, and the Earl Scruggs Review. Johnny sang "She's All I Got." The entire show is available on YouTube and is well worth watching.

I want to mention the travel required to perform that show. On August 23, they performed an afternoon show at Carowinds Amusement Park in Charlotte, NC. After the show, they boarded a flight to Los Angeles to do *The Midnight Special* on the evening of August 24. They spent the night in L.A. before flying back east for a show in Manitowoc, WI, on August 25. What an exhausting schedule.

On October 25, Johnny and the boys played in Greenfield at the Third Annual Toys For Tots benefit program at the McClain High School Auditorium.

A week later, Johnny's latest single, "Song and Dance Man," was released and went all the way to number 8 on the Billboard Country Chart. This marked his seventh consecutive chart single and fifth in the Top 10. They closed out 1973 with a New Year's Eve show in New Orleans at Riverside Music Hall. It had been a great year for Johnny Paycheck and The Lovemakers.

Chapter 29

The Don Markham Incident

In late 1973, Johnny Paycheck reached out to Dave Gray to discuss the possibility of his band, the Bakersfield Brass, opening for him at selected shows across the country.

The Bakersfield Brass formed in the early 1960s and performed alongside Buck Owens. Over the years, the band experienced several lineup changes. By 1973, its members included Dave Gray, Don Markham, and others. They often performed under the name "Dave Gray and the Bakersfield Brass," with Dave serving as the lead vocalist and trumpet player.

Dave and his bandmates were intrigued by the idea of collaborating with Johnny, so they accepted his offer. Their first joint appearance likely took place on October 25, 1973, in Greenfield, OH, during Paycheck's annual Toys For Tots benefit show.

After a few more collaborative performances, Johnny extended another offer to Gray and Markham, inviting them to join his show and perform on stage with him and the band. Once again, Gray and Markham accepted the invitation. They changed their name to the Tennessee Trumpets and began touring with Johnny Paycheck and the Lovemakers in January 1974, starting with shows in Texas. The performances were typically billed as "Johnny Paycheck and the Lovemakers featuring Don Adams, with the Tennessee Trumpets also appearing," or similar wording. Although they were occasionally referred to as the Bakersfield Brass, they were no longer officially recognized by that name.

After spending most of January performing one-night shows at clubs and dance halls across Texas, the Johnny Paycheck Show made a stop in Scottsbluff, Nebraska, before heading east for performances in Georgia, Florida, and Pennsylvania. Notable highlights from this tour included a show on February 7 at the Imperial Room in Tampa, Florida, featuring Johnny Russell, and another performance on February 16 at a package show in Chambersburg, Pennsylvania, featuring Jeanne Pruitt.

On February 21, they performed at the Golden Nugget Casino in Las Vegas for the opening night of a six-night engagement.

In 1974, the expansive Golden Nugget Showroom had not yet been built, so performances were held in the lounge, which had an intimate setting and could seat approximately 250 people. Johnny was scheduled to perform multiple shows each night, with the last show ending around one o'clock in the morning.

On the final night, February 26, the band was preparing for the grueling twenty-eight-hour drive to Dayton, OH, where they were scheduled to perform on February 28. After showering and packing their bags, Don and Gary returned to the lounge and sat at a table near the stage to watch a young singer perform. Just a couple of minutes into the performance, the bus driver caught Don's attention from a short distance and told him he needed to get his gear on the bus, as they were preparing to depart.

Don signaled to the bus driver to wait a moment, as he and the other musicians didn't want to leave in the middle of a song, which is considered rude and unprofessional among musicians. In response, the bus driver threw Don's room keys towards their table, hitting Don in the face. This infuriated Don.

As soon as the performer finished his song, Don got up and headed straight to the lobby, where the bus driver was standing. Without hesitation, Don punched the bus driver hard in the face, sending him sprawling to the floor, breaking his glasses, and causing a deep cut above his eye. A police officer, who happened to be nearby, witnessed the entire incident. He looked at Don and said, "You'd better get your ass out of here."

Don left the bus driver lying on the floor and went to his room to grab his bags. On his way, he encountered Johnny heading to the lobby and told him what had happened. Johnny then went to the lobby and found the bus driver sitting in a chair by the door. To avoid trouble, Johnny gave the bus driver an undisclosed amount of money and arranged for a taxi to the airport. He even retrieved the driver's belongings from the bus and loaded them into the taxi for him. It remains unclear when or where the bus driver managed to clean himself up. Fortunately for Don, he never heard anything else about the incident and they never saw that bus driver again.

Reflecting on the situation, Don recalled, "I was rooming with Paycheck at the time, and the bus driver had already moved John's belongings onto the bus. He could have moved mine too, just like he had done before, but for some reason, he wanted to be a prick that night."

During my interview with Don about the incident, he described the bus driver as a "weird son of a bitch." When I asked him to explain further, Don said the driver tended to approach people sitting and massage their shoulders. Don found this behavior intrusive and warned the bus driver, "Keep your goddamned hands off me."

It seemed to me that Don was looking for an opportunity to confront the bus driver, and getting hit in the face with his keys might have been that opportunity.

A few hours later, a significant incident took place that would have a lasting impact on country music. Trumpet player Don Markham was reluctantly pressed into service as a bus driver following the incident at the Golden Nugget. Markham stopped to refuel the bus at a truck stop east of Albuquerque, New Mexico. While most of the band remained on the bus asleep, a couple of members, including Johnny, went inside the truck stop.

As the bus was being fueled, another tour bus pulled in. It belonged to Merle Haggard. Markham, who was not particularly happy about performing with Johnny Paycheck, saw this as a positive sign. He walked over to Haggard's bus and asked the driver if Haggard was on board. The driver confirmed he was, so Markham requested to see him. Haggard was awake, and after checking with him, the driver invited Markham aboard.

Inside, Markham found Haggard and steel guitarist Norm Hamlet sitting together, talking.

In a February 27, 2017, article published on *The Boot.com*, Hamlet described Markham's frustrations. "These guys (referring to the Adams Boys) are fighting all the time, and it's driving me crazy," Markham said. Then he asked Haggard for a job with his band, the Strangers. Without much hesitation, Haggard agreed. So, Markham unloaded his belongings from Johnny's bus and loaded them onto Haggard's.

"Don (Markham) joined us right then and there," Hamlet recalled. "We didn't have any horns at the time. It was just guitars. So, he was a great addition," he added.

Johnny was irritated by the thought of losing a band member under those conditions, but he was okay with Markham leaving because money was tight, and he was struggling to pay the bills.

Don was relieved to see Markham leave, stating, "He was never a good fit for our band. He was always nervous and rarely talked to anyone. He was a good musician, but his personality just didn't fit in."

As news of Markham's transition from Paycheck to Haggard circulated throughout Nashville, details emerged claiming that the Adams boys had assaulted their bus driver. However, this was not entirely accurate.

"The Adams Boys didn't beat up the bus driver," Don clarified. "Don Adams beat up the bus driver, and the son of a bitch had it coming."

After Don Markham departed, Dave Gray became the only remaining member of the Tennessee Trumpets and became a competent bus driver as well. He transitioned into The Lovemakers, and the Tennessee Trumpets were history.

Chapter 30

Hard Working Ernie Stepp

According to nearly everyone I've spoken with, if Ernie Stepp were your friend, he would treat you like a brother. Don Adams, Steve Marple, and Ralph May all confirmed that if Ernie liked you, he'd do anything in the world for you. If you crossed him, though. Well, that was a different story because Ernie was a very tough man and by all accounts, almost fearless.

Ernie's official job title was bodyguard, but in reality, he also acted as an enforcer, a debt collector, and a quasi-road manager. He took all of those jobs seriously, and sometimes that led to hard times, not for Ernie, but for whoever crossed him.

I'll give you two examples to illustrate. Please note that I don't know exactly when these incidents occurred; I only know they occurred between 1972 and 1975.

Late one night after a show, Don was sitting in the club owner's office, waiting to be paid. After what seemed to

Don like a long wait, the club owner entered the office and handed Don a check.

Don reminded the club owner that Johnny didn't accept checks. In fact, Johnny's contract with every small venue he performed at specified that he was to be paid in cash.

The club owner said, "That's too bad," and escorted Don to the door.

Don handed the club owner back his check and went to the bus to inform Johnny about what had happened. As Don was talking, another man, who turned out to be the club owner's brother, knocked on the bus door. Dave Gray opened the door, and the man stepped onto the bus, handed the check to Don, and said, "You forgot this."

That's when Ernie grabbed hold of the man and said, "We don't take checks, motherfucker. You'd better get us some cash out here right now, or you're going to take a ride up the road with us, and you won't be walking back. Do you understand me? Now, you holler up there and tell that other asshole to bring the cash out."

Ernie then took the man by his collar and walked him halfway back towards the club, where he stopped and told the man to holler at the club owner and tell him to bring the cash. The man did as he was told, and Ernie walked him back to the bus. A few minutes later, the club owner brought an envelope of cash to the bus. After Don counted the money and confirmed it was all there. Ernie released his hostage, and the bus drove off.

Another time, Johnny was performing a show at an Army base inside an airplane hangar. During the show, an intoxicated man walked down in front of the stage and stood looking up at Johnny and the band. The man pointed his finger at Johnny and said, "You suck!" Then he pointed at each band member and told them they all sucked, too.

Un-phased, Johnny turned to Ernie, who was standing somewhere offstage, and nodded before pointing to the man down front. Taking that as his cue, Ernie took off at full speed towards the man who didn't see Ernie coming.

Ernie clotheslined the man so hard that he nearly completed a full circle in mid-air before hitting the ground. Ernie then proceeded to drag the man over to a large open door overlooking a loading dock and gave him a couple of extra shots, leaving the man lying on the floor unable to get up.

Ernie then turned to Ralph May, who had been following behind, and said: "Grab his feet, Ralph."

Ernie and Ralph then proceeded to throw the man out the open door and into a snow drift, where he presumably spent the rest of the show.

Chapter 31

Misadventures

Riding High

The boys started 1974 with a televised appearance in Toronto on *The Ian Tyson Show*, a weekly broadcast show that aired every Thursday night on CTV Television.

They began their touring schedule in Texas on January 12 with a show in Bryan, followed by a two-night stint in Corsicana. They then zigzagged across the country for the next several weeks with stops in Iowa, Nebraska, Pennsylvania, Florida, and Georgia before heading to Las Vegas for their ill-fated six-night engagement.

On March 17, they accomplished a feat that I'm not sure has ever been replicated. Due to a scheduling snafu, Johnny was booked for shows in two different cities: a 2:00 PM show at the Greensboro Coliseum in Greensboro, NC, and an 8:00 PM show at the Cumberland County Memorial Arena in Fayetteville, NC. They ended up playing both shows, separated only by a 95-mile bus ride. Don confirmed that this actually happened, noting that there was discussion about possibly canceling one of the shows. However, Johnny insisted on performing both so as not to disappoint his fans.

In early May, there was some unexpected turnover in the band. While taking a break at a rest stop in Florida, Johnny looked out the bus window and saw drummer Lonnie Nance buying marijuana from a young man who was later identified as the son of a Florida state trooper. (I'm not sure how that information came to light, but that's what Don told me when he shared the story.)

Johnny was sober at that time, and while he might have overlooked some of the band's private activities, he could not ignore a drug transaction taking place publicly by one of his band members in a parking lot just a few feet from his bus. Consequently, Johnny fired Lonnie and replaced him with a drummer he knew named Jimmy Stewart. It isn't known whether Johnny fired him on the spot or waited until the end of the tour, and Don couldn't remember. I suspect it was at the end of the tour, as it would be tough to replace your drummer while out on the road.

I suspect this occurred sometime in the first half of May. I say this because on May 1, they played a show at The Big Still Knight Club in Fort Myers. I found a photo from that performance, and Lonnie is clearly visible. I also have a bootleg tape of a Johnny Paycheck show at the Hunter's Lodge near Fairfax, VA. Johnny introduces the band during that show, and the drummer is Jimmy Stewart. That exact date of that show is unknown, but it was sometime in the latter half of May.

In the midst of a busy touring schedule, Johnny took the time to play a benefit show on May 11 in Sabina, OH, for a 7-year-old boy named Trent Newman. Trent was the son of

Mr. and Mrs. Tom Newman of Sabina, and he was battling cancer.

The show was held in the school gymnasium in Sabina, in front of a standing-room-only crowd of over 1,100 people. By all accounts, Johnny, despite battling a severe sore throat, delivered a spectacular performance, as did Don and the rest of the band. The show raised over $3,000 for young Trent and his family.

Don was still riding high from the success of his album and was now receiving enhanced billing in advertisements for Johnny's shows. Many of the ads that I have seen mention Don prominently with things like "Johnny Paycheck and the Lovemakers featuring Don Adams," Johnny Paycheck with Don Adams," and even "Johnny Paycheck and Don Adams."

Hoping to build on Don's momentum, Atlantic released a new record, "Baby Let Your Long Hair Down," as a single. The record is credited as "Don Adams and The Greenfield Express." The Greenfield Express was really The Lovemakers band with Don's brother, Farrell, filling in on bass." The record reached number 80 on the Billboard Country Chart.

In August, Atlantic released another single from Don. This one was "That's Love," a song written by Gary and Don. The song shot quickly up the charts, and Don was encouraged to form a band and buy a bus.

"They told me that it was going to be a top-five hit and I needed to form a band and get ready to go on the road," Don said. "I didn't have the money to buy a bus or pay for a band, but I thought I could figure it out somehow."

I asked Don if he intended to take members of the Lovemakers to form his band.

"That was the plan. I knew I could get Gary to play guitar and Steve to play drums. I figured I could probably get Doug on steel. As for bass, I thought about adding Farrell. I thought they might give me a little time to get enough money rolling in to start paying them," Don said before adding with a smile, "They were my friends and family, you know."

Then the unbelievable happened. Atlantic Records, which had been losing money on its country music venture, closed its doors without warning. With their closing, there was no promotion or distribution for the record, so it stalled on the charts at number 52, and all hope for a breakout hit faded into dust.

The disappointment wore on Don, but he and the rest of the band soldiered on. They played in front of big crowds in cities across the United States and Canada, with shows in Chicago, Toronto, Indianapolis, Philadelphia, Memphis, Phoenix, Miami, Seattle, Vancouver, and various points in between. Saying that Johnny Paycheck and The Lovemakers were one of the hottest tickets in America wasn't a stretch a t all.

Sometime in the late Fall, there was an incident that, had it gotten out of control, could have spelled disaster.

Neither Johnny nor Don was happy with drummer Jimmy Stewart. According to Don, Stewart liked to drink, and on several occasions, he drank to the point of not being able to perform up to par. He had fallen off his stool at one show and had to leave the stage and throw up at another. Finally, Johnny told Don to fire Stewart and hire a new drummer.

Don's plan was to finish out the tour and fire Stewart after the last show. Plans changed, though, when, after a show in Fairborn, OH, Stewart became intoxicated and had to be helped to his room when they returned to their hotel.

The next morning, the band, minus Stewart, gathered for breakfast and loaded their bags on the bus. Unsure where he was, Don went to Stewart's room and found the door cracked open. Don went inside and tried to rouse Stewart. After several minutes of trying, Don finally got Stewart to open his eyes and sit up on the bed. Don told him to get dressed and get his stuff on the bus, but Stewart lay back down and closed his eyes.

At that, Don, in classic Adams Boys style, took a cigarette lighter from his pocket and lit the corner of a sheet on fire. Then he exited Stewart's room, leaving the door cracked. From there, Don walked to the front office, told them he'd seen smoke coming from Stewart's room, and made his way to the bus, where he informed Johnny that Stewart was no longer with the band and wouldn't be getting on the bus. With that, the bus departed for their next show.

Apparently, there were no deaths, injuries, or fallout from Don's caper, as he never heard a word about it.

Johnny utilized club drummers and local drummers to cover the last handful of shows before breaking for Christmas. He told Don to hire a new drummer, and Don had one in mind. He put in a call to his brother-in-law, Steve Marple, who was then playing with Ralph May's band in shows all over Ohio.

Steve said he was interested, so Don arranged for a tryout in front of Johnny. Johnny hired him without reservation, and as of December 30, Steve was the Lovemakers' new drummer. His first show was on January 3, 1975, at Memorial Hall in Kansas City, KS, the site of Patsy Cline's last show in 19 63.

Gators and Midgets

In the early morning hours of a February day in 1975, while traveling through northern Florida, Steve Marple was suddenly jolted out of his bunk by a hard bump, accompanied by a loud rumbling sound and a shower of sparks. The bus came to a stop as Steve and his bandmates scrambled to their feet, rattled by what had just occurred. The fact that no one was injured is a testament to the bus driver's skill, as he kept the bus upright and on the road without colliding with any other vehicles.

Steve, who had joined the band just a couple of months prior, recalled the incident vividly during one of our interviews:

> It was around three o'clock in the morning, so we were all asleep. All of a sudden, there was a big bang, and I'm getting thrown on the floor. I could see sparks through the window, and there was a loud rumbling sound. The bus driver got it stopped, then turned around, and said, "I think a tire fell off the bus."
>
> By that time, everyone was up except John. We were all confused as Hell and kind of out of it. I remember Don and a couple of others getting off the bus with the driver to check it out, and about that time, John came staggering out from his bed in the back, shouting, "What the Hell is going on here?"
>
> I got to laughing because John's hair was sticking up in every direction, and all he was wearing was his underwear, the tighty whitey kind. He had his hands on his hips, and he's sporting a big old piss hard-on. I couldn't stop laughing, and when the other guys looked at him, they started laughing too. That pissed him off, so he went and put pants and boots on, then went outside to see what had happened.
>
> The rest of us followed him off and saw that one of the back tires was missing. We had stopped right next to a swamp. You could hear frogs croaking, and the mosquitoes were eating our butts up. I thought, *there's alligators and snakes, and who*

knows what all in there.

The bus driver took out a flashlight and shined it behind us on the road. There was a long trench, probably six inches deep, in the asphalt from the bus sliding on the rim. Then he started shining the light into the swamp, and there was that tire sticking up out of the water about fifty feet away. John looked at it and said, "Steve, go out there and get that tire."

I said, "Hell, no! Not happening, man. You don't pay me enough."

So, the bus driver takes his cowboy boots and socks off, rolls up his pant legs, and wades out into that swamp after that tire. Every time he took a step, you could hear the muck on the bottom making that sucking sound, and he's trying not to get his feet stuck. He finally makes it to the tire and starts dragging it back towards the road, and Don yells, "Watch out for that alligator!"

Well, that got the bus driver moving fast. He looked like Jesus walking on the water. When he got to the guard rail, a couple of guys pulled the tire out, and the driver came up out of there all covered with mud and stinkin' swamp water. He was pissed.

The tire was torn up pretty badly and needed to be re-placed, as did the rim, meaning they would need to get the bus worked on before they could continue their journey.

The state police arrived shortly afterward, and eventually, a heavy-duty tow truck came to take the bus to a nearby all-night truck stop for necessary repairs. While they waited, a couple of the guys went into the truck stop for coffee while the others stayed on the bus. As the sun began to rise, there was a knock on the bus door. Steve got up to see who was knocking. To his surprise, it was a young woman of short stature, often called a little person. In the vernacular of the mid-1970s, she might have been called a midget. "When I looked out the window and saw a midget knocking on the door, it surprised me. You see, I was scared of midgets. They freaked me out," Steve recalled.

Steve opened the bus door and asked, "Can I help you with something?"

"Is Johnny Paycheck on this bus?" the young woman asked.

"Yes, he is," Steve answered.

"Can I see him?" she asked.

"I'm not sure," Steve said. "Let me ask him."

Steve walked to the back of the bus, where Johnny was sleeping, and told him that a woman wanted to see him.

"How's she look? Is she pretty?" Johnny inquired.

"She looks pretty good," Steve replied.

"Well, let her come on back then."

Steve allowed the woman onto the bus and guided her to where Johnny was sleeping.

"She was there for about an hour," Steve remembered.

After she left, Johnny, who was five feet five inches tall, emerged with a sheepish grin on his face.

Don laughed and said, "Well, you finally found a woman who's shorter than you!"

Steve added, "I'm sorry, John. I forgot to mention she was a midget."

Johnny grinned and said, "It don't make one bit of difference. Let's go inside and get some breakfast."

It was almost noon when the bus was finally repaired, allowing the band to resume their journey. Just another day on the road.

Going into 1975, Johnny Paycheck, while still a big concert draw, was not selling records at nearly the pace he had grown accustomed to. His last three singles all charted, but none inside the top 10.

He still pursued an aggressive road schedule although it was entirely focussed in the eastern half of the country from January through May. It wasn't until June that he headed west where he spent a week performing several shows in Oregon and California, before heading east again to perform in Missouri, Illinois, Indiana, and Ohio. I suspect he did this as a cost cutting measure since record sales were down and he was starting to show signs of financial distress.

Even so, in early March, he had brought on Greenfield vocalist Ralph May as a part of his show. Ralph wasn't a band member, but would come onstage during Don's opening performance to do a couple songs. According to Don, Johnny's goal was to have more of a stand alone package show with multiple singers performing before he came on. In this case the vocalists were Dave Gray, Ralph, Don of course, and sometimes Gary. It;s interesting to note that Ralph told me he went to work for "rent money," and that he considered the experience gained to be worth his effort.

Farrell to the Rescue

In 1975, while on tour in the South, Florida, perhaps, or maybe the Carolinas, Don injured his back, making it too painful to stand on stage and play. He called his brother Farrell back in Greenfield, who came down and filled in, playing bass and singing harmony for Johnny for about two weeks. This marked the second time Farrell had filled in for one of his brothers while they were on the road.

A bit of trivia: Farrell is left-handed but always plays a right-handed bass.

Chapter 32

Vodka with the Killer

On March 23, 1975, The Johnny Paycheck Show rolled into Chicago for a performance at the International Amphitheater. The event was promoted as "Country In The City," with the headlining act being the legendary Jerry Lee Lewis, famously nicknamed "The Killer." In addition to Lewis, the lineup featured Johnny Paycheck and the Lovemakers, veteran performer Ferlin Husky, 16-year-old rising star Tanya Tucker, and Eddie Rabbitt, who was virtually unknown at the time. Although Rabbitt was not originally scheduled to perform, he was added in anticipation of his debut album, set to be released that August.

Two performances were scheduled: a matinee show at 1:30 PM and an evening show at 6:30 PM. A single ticket was valid for both shows, with Jerry Lee Lewis performing only in the second show. Eddie Rabbitt was the opening act, followed by Ferlin Husky. The Lovemakers accompanied both artists. After Husky, Johnny Paycheck would take the stage, and Tanya Tucker, who was still enjoying the success of her 1974 album, *Would You Lay With Me (In A Field Of Stone)*, and its number-one title track, would close the first show. The schedule would remain the same for the second show, except that Jerry Lee Lewis would perform after Tucker to close the evening's performances.

The mood that day was somber for the band, as steel guitar player Doug Jerningan was leaving to join the renowned bluegrass fiddle player Vassar Clements, making this his last performance with The Lovemakers. Everyone was saddened to see Doug go, especially Gary, who was absolutely distraught. He and Doug had forged a close friendship and professional bond since they began playing together in 1965. Over the years, they had performed hundreds of shows together, collaborated as songwriters, recorded an album, and developed a distinct sound that contributed to The Lovemakers' reputation as country music's top touring band.

In preparation for Doug's departure, steel guitarist Wayne Hobbs, who had previously played with Barbara Mandrell's band, the Do Rites, spent two weeks traveling with the Paycheck Show. During this time, he recorded Doug's performances and practiced with Gary to become familiar with Johnny's songs and the band's style, in an effort to make the transition as smooth as possible.

Ralph May recalled the episode vividly. "Gary and Wayne would practice in their hotel room during the day, trying to get Doug's licks down. You see, Doug and Gary had a whole thing going. They were featured players on stage. I mean, they had all kinds of things worked out."

Johnny had so much confidence in Gary and Doug that he granted them great creative flexibility on stage, as long as it did not interfere with his performance.

Ralph continued, "So, Gary and Wayne would sit in their room and practice for a couple of hours each day, then Gary would come down to the lobby or bar, or wherever we were hanging out, and tell us how great Wayne was doing. He'd say, 'Boys, Lightnin' is really settin' 'em up today.' I asked him what he meant, and he'd say, 'Oh, man. He's faster than Doug.' That statement had us all chuckling and shaking our heads because we couldn't believe it."

Because of Gary's boasting, Don began referring to Wayne as "Lightnin' Bread" to the delight of the rest of the band. By 1975, Doug Jernigan was widely recognized as one of the fastest steel guitar players of all time. He may have been the first to perform solos at speeds comparable to those of banjo and fiddle players. This recognition does not diminish Wayne Hobbs's talent; he was an exceptional steel guitar player in his own right, having performed with several renowned artists, including Jerry Lee Lewis, Marty Robbins, and Barbara Mandrell. However, claiming that he was faster than Doug Jernigan is simply not true.

A near-capacity crowd attended the show that evening. Eddie Rabbitt, accompanied by The Lovemakers, opened the event with a performance that lasted about 20 minutes.

Following Rabbitt was Ferlin Husky, who received an enthusiastic welcome from the audience. The band kicked off the first song, "Just for You," which had been a top 10 hit in 1967. As the song began, Husky began stomping his foot and slapping his hand on his guitar to signal the band to increase the tempo. This was a common practice for him during live performances, and he likely did so on this occasion to make the song sound livelier in response to the crowd's warm reception. However, Husky often struggled to sing at the tempo he set, whether it was too slow or too fast. When this occurred, he would stop the song, instruct the band to speed it up or slow it down, and typically make comments that led the audience to believe the band had made a mistake. This habit greatly irritated Don and was a primary reason he disliked playing for Ferlin Husky. True to form, after Husky had the band pick up the tempo, he flubbed his opening and immediately fell behind. As expected, he stopped the song, turned to Don, and loudly declared for those in the first few rows to hear, "You're playing too fast. Slow it down!"

Don was livid and shot back, "Oh no! YOU set the tempo. If you set the tempo, then you'd better be able to sing it that way. Pull that shit again, and I'll knock your ass off the end of this stage!"

Husky gritted his teeth and started to say something back, but stopped himself. Finally, he said, "Kick it off again!"

The band started the song at the same tempo as the record. Husky sang it perfectly, and the rest of the set went smoothly.

Next up was the Johnny Paycheck Show, and as usual, trumpet player Dave Gray started it off with a couple of vocal numbers before Don stepped up to the mic and did a twenty-minute set of original songs and covers. Gary and Doug then performed an instrumental number. Finally, Don called Ralph May out to sing one or two songs before doing one more himself.

Only then did Don introduce Johnny, "Now, ladies and gentlemen, please welcome to the stage, Epic recording artist, Johnny Paycheck!" As Johnny came on stage, the band played the theme song from the movie *Shaft*. Gary and Doug had arranged the instrumental to make a seamless transition into Johnny's opening number.

The crowd gave Johnny a thunderous applause and he launched into some of his biggest hits, including "Don't Take Her She's All I Got," "Mr. Lovemaker," "Someone to Give My Love to," and "Song and Dance Man," as well as his current single, "Loving You Beats All I've Ever Seen."

Johnny called on Gary to perform a number in the middle of his set. It's likely that Gary would have performed an uptempo version of a popular song, such as "Gentle On My Mind" or a similar song. Gary was a good singer, but he often sacrificed his vocal performance to highlight his impeccable guitar skills. He would hurry through the lyrics, while his fingers moved at lightning speed over the strings. The crowd would eat it up, and Gary would grin widely before taking a bow. Johnny would then walk back to the mic, smiling and shaking his head, and finish the set.

When they were finished, the crowd responded with a standing ovation as Johnny left the stage. The Lovemakers played a short instrumental outro and then exited the stage as well. They were hitting on all cylinders and had put on an excellent performance.

As the band left the stage, Gary glanced up at Jerry Lee's VIP suite, which was situated on the second level beside the stage. Jerry Lee was looking down, smiling at the band. Gary nudged Don to look up as well, and when Don did, Jerry Lee raised his glass in a gesture of approval towards the Lovemakers.

That's when things started to spin off the rails.

When they arrived at their dressing room, a member of Jerry Lee's entourage came in and invited Johnny and The Lovemakers to Jerry Lee's private VIP suite to relax. Everyone except Johnny accepted the invitation. Johnny didn't have a favorable opinion of Jerry Lee at the time because of a disagreement they had over hotel rooms after a package show they performed together a few years earlier.

the Lovemakers made their way up to Jerry Lee's suite while Tanya Tucker's band conducted its sound check in preparation for her performance. Upon arriving at the door, they noticed two Chicago firemen standing in the hallway outside. It was unclear what they were doing. Perhaps they were inspecting fire extinguishers or ensuring that emergency exits were unobstructed. Nobody knew for sure.

The member of Jerry Lee's entourage then knocked on the VIP suite's door. The small window, reminiscent of a speakeasy, slid open, and an eye appeared from the other side. "Shit! The cops are outside!" a voice shouted from behind the door.

There was a minor ruckus inside, then the original eye was replaced by a different eye, and a voice, recognizable as that of Jerry Lee Lewis, exclaimed, "What the hell do they want now? They already tore my goddamn airplane apart."

"Those aren't cops! They're firemen!" Ralph May shouted at the window.

"Firemen? What the hell do they want?"

The firemen, slightly confused by the situation, shrugged. One of them remarked, "We don't want anything."

"They don't want anything," Ralph echoed.

With that, the small window slid shut, and the door opened. The Lovemakers were welcomed inside while the firemen walked away, likely wondering what had just transpired.

Once inside, the guys were lined up side by side, just inside the door, and all started to wonder what was going on. Ralph was standing farthest from the door; thus, he was closest to the room's occupants. Next to him was Don. Filling out the line in some order were Gary, Steve Marple, Dave Gray, Paul Justice, and Doug Jernigan.

Ralph took a pack of cigarettes from his pocket and offered one to Don before taking one for himself. As they lit their cigarettes, Jerry Lee approached them from across the room. He walked up to Ralph, extended his hand, and said, "Do you mind if I grab a cigarette from you?"

"Sure," Ralph answered, shaking Jerry Lee's hand before handing him a cigarette.

Jerry Lee took the cigarette, examined it, and said, "What kind of cigarette is this?"

"It's just a regular cigarette."

"It's not wacky tobacky, is it?"

"No, it's not wacky tobacky. It just has a hole in the filter for some reason."

According to Ralph, they had been in North Carolina a few days earlier when Johnny gave him and Steve Marple $100 and instructed them to buy as many cigarettes as they could. North Carolina is a major tobacco-producing state, making cigarettes significantly less expensive there than in most other states. Ralph and Steve managed to purchase two large grocery sacks of Vantage-brand cigarettes, enough to keep them supplied for at least a few weeks. Vantage cigarettes are unique because they have a hole in the filter designed to reduce the amount of tar and nicotine that smokers inhale. It was this hole in the filter that caught Jerry Lee's attention and prompted him to ask Ralph if they were smoking "wacky tobacky" (marijuana).

Ralph lit Jerry Lee's cigarette, and Jerry Lee moved down the line to Don. Looking Don up and down, Jerry Lee turned back to Ralph and asked, "Well, who's this squirrel?" while gesturing to Don.

Hearing that, Ralph thought, *My God, what are you doing calling Don a squirrel? There's gonna be trouble. You're gonna get your head knocked off if you don't shut up.*

Don gave Jerry Lee a terse look, then smiled and extended his hand, saying, "I'm Don Adams."

Jerry Lee shook Don's hand and said, "I know who you are, Don. Don't pay any attention to anything I say; I didn't mean anything by it."

"I know you didn't. It's nice to meet you," Don replied.

Did Jerry Lee already know Don? He at least knew of him. Everyone in country music had heard of Don Adams by 1975.

After making his way through the receiving line and greeting all his guests, Jerry Lee invited everyone inside to relax.

He ordered drinks for the group and encouraged them to help themselves to the buffet.

Jerry Lee and his entourage had arrived at the Amphitheater that afternoon in a convoy of a dozen white Cadillacs. According to Ralph, two of Jerry Lee's wives, one current and one former, were present, and he was ordering them around and telling them what to do. Several children, grandchildren, and other family members were also there, along with his manager and a large group of hangers-on that rivaled the size and appearance of Elvis Presley's Memphis Mafia.

Jerry Lee sat down at a large round table in the center of the room and began pouring glasses of vodka from three bottles that one of his wives had brought. Soon, several people gathered around the table, including Don, Gary, Dave Gray, Paul Justice, and a few members of Jerry Lee's entourage. The conversation started with Jerry Lee sharing stories about growing up with his cousins: country singer Mickey Gilley and evangelist Jimmy Swaggart.

Before long, Jerry Lee pulled out his Bible, and the discussion shifted to religion. Dave, who had once been a Pentecostal preacher (though he had definitely strayed from that path by this point in his life), joined in. Don and Gary had grown up in the Pentecostal Church and still held on to their faith, albeit somewhat loosely at times. Their mother, Kate, was known for praying over the sick and injured, reportedly healing many, and she possessed the gift of speaking in tongues. This set the stage for a deep discussion about Christianity, which likely became quite spirited, judging by the number of vodka glasses consumed.

Ralph and Steve sat nearby, smoking cigarettes and listening to the conversation. After a short time, they left in pursuit of Tanya Tucker, who, by then, had finished her performance and gone back to her dressing room. They found her sitting with her father on a couch outside her dressing room. Ralph and Steve tried to talk to Tanya, but she was standoffish and gave them no attention.

"Tanya was wearing a red jumpsuit like Elvis wore, and she looked really good," Ralph recalled. "She wouldn't talk to me and Marple for nothing in the world. And her dad was hanging close to her."

After getting nowhere with Tanya, Ralph and Steve made their way back to the dressing room, where the band had started to gather in preparation for the next show. Everyone was present, except for Gary, and no one knew where he was. Seeing Ralph and Steve come through the door, Johnny asked them if they had seen Gary. Ralph told Johnny that the last time they saw him, he was with Jerry Lee, studying the Bible and drinking vodka. Johnny asked Ralph if he would try to find him, as it was getting close to show time.

Ralph went out again to look for Gary and spotted him sitting under the stage. "I was standing in the aisle, several rows back, when I noticed Gary sitting on the floor in front of the stage with his head on his knees. He was drunk. Real drunk. Stumbling drunk," Ralph recalled. "I got him to his feet, and he was crying and going on about Doug leaving. I told him he needed to get ready to go on, and I started walking him back to the dressing room. He could barely walk, and he just kept going on and on about Doug."

By the time Ralph brought Gary back to the dressing room, the band had already gone on stage to set up and conduct their soundcheck. Johnny glanced at Gary and said, "Ralph, keep an eye on him. I'm going to get some coffee going."

Ralph was helping Gary straighten his clothes and comb his hair so he would look presentable on stage. When Johnny returned, Gary saw him and said, "I'm sorry, John. Someone gave me something up there. I don't know what happened."

"I understand, Gary," Johnny said. "I ain't mad at ya or nothin'. You boys used to put up with a lot from me, too. Me and George. All of us were crazy back then."

Turning to Ralph, Johnny said, "Ralph, I gotta get ready to go on. You stay here and give him all the coffee he can take. I'm gonna tell Don to let me call you out after I sing a song or two. When I do, you bring Gary with you and drop him off at his amp on your way to the microphone."

Ralph continued to give Gary coffee and directed him to the restroom to empty his bladder of the vodka and coffee he had consumed. When Johnny called Ralph to come out and sing, Ralph scooped up Gary and his guitar and made his way to the stage.

"The stage was twenty-five feet high, and you had to run up a ramp to reach it," Ralph recalled. "Gary was wobbling all over the place, and I was afraid he would fall off the side, so I hurried him along as quickly as I could to get him into position."

Ralph got Gary where he was supposed to be, and Gary promptly sat down on his amp. Ralph got him back on his feet and said, "You can't do that. You gotta stand up, man."

"Gary was unsteady on his feet, and I was afraid he was going to trip over his foot pedals," Ralph recalled. "Gary looked at me and said, 'What's going on, Ralph? Soundcheck?' I handed him his guitar and said, You missed the soundcheck. You're in the show now.'"

Once Gary was settled in, Ralph went up to the microphone and performed two songs: a cover of Chuck Berry's "Promised Land" and "Ol' 55" by Eagles. Throughout his performance, Ralph frequently glanced over at Gary, worried that he might fall off the stage. Fortunately, Gary got control of himself, everything went smoothly, and they finished the show without any problems.

After the show concluded, Johnny and the band boarded their bus and hit the road on I-65 heading toward Nashville. Dave Gray was at the wheel, and, at some point during the journey, all the band members, except for Gary, gathered near the front of the bus to smoke cigarettes and chat. Suddenly, Gary, who had been sleeping in his bunk, rolled out and made his way to join the others at the front.

"He looked like Hell," Ralph recalled. "All he was wearing was his underwear. His eyes were bloodshot, and his hair was going in every direction."

Don glanced at him as he made his way to the front of the bus and said, "Gary, what the hell happened to you?'

Gary looked around, confused, and replied, "What? What do you mean?"

Don shot back, "Why look at you. You've shit yourself!"

In July, Johnny and the band returned to Greenfield to perform at the Greene Country Town Festival. They gave two outdoor shows on the McCalin High School Athletic Field. One on July 18 and one on July 19. As far as I can determine, this was Johnny's first show in Greenfield, other than his annual Toys For Tots benefit shows, since Valentine's Day, 1962.

A very important side note to these two shows is the return of steel guitarist Doug Jernigan to the band.

Chapter 33

Roger and Wayne in Los Vegas

Johnny Paycheck and the Lovemakers arrived in Las Vegas, Nevada, on September 14, 1975, for a three-week engagement at the Landmark Hotel. This marked their first return to Sin City since Don had an altercation with their bus driver a year and a half earlier.

The schedule was intense: two shows every night, seven nights a week, which was typical for headline performers of that era. During our interview, Don mentioned several times that he believed the band's performances over those three weeks in Las Vegas were the best they had ever done.

"There was always something special about playing in Vegas," Don said. "The atmosphere, lights, everyone dressed up. There were people from all over the world there. It just made you want to do your best. It was a good feeling."

Don was not alone in his opinion. The legendary performer Wayne Newton, a well-known figure in Las Vegas who regularly performed at venues like the Desert Inn, The

Frontier, and the Sands Hotel and Casino, heard about Johnny's show and decided to attend one evening.

After the show, Newton went backstage to meet Johnny and the band and to congratulate them on a fantastic performance. After posing for several photos, he told Johnny, "You have the best band in Las Vegas."

Don Adams and Steve Marple told me, separately, in interviews, that they considered it a huge compliment coming from someone like Wayne Newton.

Don Adams Circa 1975 Courtesy of Steve Marple

At some point during this Las Vegas trip, Johnny's wife surprised him with a gift: a brand-new pair of platform shoes. Don described them as having "5-inch heels," though this was likely an exaggeration, as most men's platform shoes typically had 3-inch heels. Nevertheless, even 3-inch heels would significantly enhance Johnny's height, as he stood only 5 feet 5 inches tall.

On the second or third night, Don completed his solo portion of the show, and the band began playing Johnny's introduction. Don then introduced Johnny, saying, "Ladies and gentlemen, please welcome to the stage, Epic recording star, Johnny Paycheck!"

As Johnny stepped onto the stage, Don turned to look, and what he saw made him burst out laughing. Johnny was wearing the platform shoes his wife had given him instead of his usual cowboy boots. Don said:

> When John came out, he had those platform shoes on, and he didn't know how to walk in them. He was walking like Frankenstein with his legs all stiff. I tried not to laugh but couldn't hold it back. I was laughing so hard that I quit playing and bent over with my hands on my knees. The other guys turned to look, and they all started laughing too. Pretty soon, the crowd started laughing. They couldn't see John. They just got to laughing at us. John stopped in his tracks and looked down at his shoes. Without saying a word, he turned and walked back down the steps to the dressing room, changed into his boots, made his way back on stage, and started singing as if nothing had happened.

I asked Don if Johnny ever wore the shoes again after that. "Nope!" Don said. "I never saw those shoes again."

Johnny always traveled with a bodyguard, and for several years, that bodyguard had been Ernie Stepp. However, during this time, Ernie was on hiatus for reasons unknown. Some people say that Johnny fired him, but I have my doubts. Ernie was not the type to simply accept being fired, so I assume his absence was due to a mutual agreement with Johnny.

Johnny's new bodyguard was his friend and the Adams boys' cousin, Roger Dillard, from Greenfield, Ohio. Where else, huh?

Roger was a bona fide tough guy, a black belt who would later take on a Mountain Man persona and perform a show at Silver Dollar City theme park, later renamed Dollywood, in Pigeon Forge, TN. He would also go on to appear in several television shows, including *The Bob Braun Show*, *That's Incredible*, and *Dollywood: A Memory Worth Repeating*, among others, and in movies: *Attica* (1974), *Brubaker* (1980), and *Those Lips, Those Eyes* (1980).

Steve Marple told me that Roger Dillard was the only man Ernie Stepp did not want to fight. "It wouldn't have gone well for Ernie," Steve said.

Roger had additional responsibilities beyond being Johnny's bodyguard. He was also tasked with training Johnny and the band in karate. Roger took this role very seriously and insisted that his students do the same.

"Roger would come around early in the morning and pound on our doors," Don said. "We had to go out behind the hotel and do stretches and exercises. Then he'd make us run in the desert. After that, we'd eat breakfast, then we would train for a couple of hours."

I asked Don if he enjoyed it.

"I sure as hell didn't enjoy getting up at six in the morning after playing music until one in the morning," Don said.

Steve remembered one morning when Don rebelled against Roger's training regimen. "We were going outside, and Don was grumpy as hell. He was trying to smoke a cigarette, and Roger told us to start running. Well, old Don took off, and he was still smoking. He smoked about a hundred cigarettes a day then. We ran twenty feet or so, and Don said, 'Fuck this! He'll just have to kick my ass, cause I ain't running no more.' He turned around, went back to his room, and got in bed. The next morning, he was back running again."

Don added, "The training part was kinda cool. He'd teach us some moves, then we'd take turns sparring with him. He told us to go after him full speed. He wanted us to try to kick him and hit him. If he thought you were holding back, he'd hit you pretty hard and tell you to pick it up. I thought I was pretty good at kicking, and I was a lot taller than Roger. So, one day, towards the end of the gig, I thought I would stand away from him and try to kick him in the head. First, I tried a couple of punches, and he blocked them, so I went to kick him. Well, he came down with his arm to block it, and when he did, he broke my toe."

I asked Don if that hurt.

Don's reply was, "Hell yes, it hurt! I couldn't stand on it, so I had to sit on a stool during the show."

Steve takes great delight in remembering Don sitting on his stool playing bass and singing harmony.

"He sat on that stool, and his foot was all bandaged up. He was just wearing a sock with no shoe. I sat back there at my drums and couldn't stop laughing."

I asked Don if Johnny participated in the karate training or if he just made the band do it.

"John did it with us. He got real good at it, too. Better than any of the rest of us. That's how he was, though. He was one of those people who could do almost anything. Things came easy to him. That's why he could not only play just about any instrument, but he could play them extremely well. He was a natural."

Roger's third job was to act as Johnny's proxy gambler. Johnny had heard from someone who worked at the casino that a particular slot machine was due for a significant payout. On the first day, Johnny played the machine for a while before trying out other games. Still hopeful for that big payout, he paid Roger $10 an hour and gave him $100 a day to play that slot machine on his behalf. As a bonus, Roger was allowed to keep any payout of $5 or less. Unfortunately, the slot machine never delivered the large payout that Johnny had hoped for. However, it did produce enough small payouts for Roger to collect a nice bonus.

"Roger left Las Vegas with more money than any of us," Don recalled.

On the morning of their departure, everyone gathered for breakfast except for Roger. Noticing that he was absent, Don asked Gary to go up to Roger's room and tell him the bus was pulling out at eight thirty, so if he wanted breakfast, he had better get down there and eat it.

Gary did as Don asked, and Roger replied that he was going for a run and that the bus could pick him up on the way out of town. Roger asked Gary to make sure his bags made it on the bus, and then he took off to go on a run.

Gary relayed Roger's message to Don, who thought it was strange but nevertheless told everyone to get their bags on the bus and get ready to ride.

Dave Gray was driving when the bus pulled out and headed for Nashville. They had driven about five miles when they spotted Roger, who was practically sprinting down the road. Dave pulled the bus over to the shoulder and opened the door. Roger hopped on the bus, and they continued on their way.

According to Don, the bus pulled into a truck stop just outside of Las Vegas to fuel up for the long ride to Nashville. Johnny got off the bus and walked inside. Within a minute, he came back out to the bus and asked Don for a dollar. Don gave him a dollar, and Johnny went back inside the truck stop. When Johnny came back to the bus, he had a big smile on his face. He had fed Don's dollar into the slot machine inside the truck stop and won a hundred dollars.

I asked Don if Johnny paid him back his dollar.

Don looked at me over his glasses and said, "Nope."

Chapter 34

The Outlaw Turn

Johnny Pulls a Greenfield

All American Man

By September, Johnny had released two singles from his newest album, *Loving You Beats All I've Ever Seen*, and neither had made much headway on the Billboard Country Charts. The title track peaked at number 26, while the follow-up, "I Don't Love Her Anymore," only reached number 38. To say that Johnny desperately needed a hit was an understatement of epic proportions, and he thought he may have found one.

Johnny and Gary had co-written a song called "All American Man," an unabashed direct counter to the women's lib movement that had overtaken the country. Knowing the song would cause controversy, Johnny decided to record it as a single and release it, figuring the publicity, good or bad, would ignite record sales and get things going again.

The song was released on Labor Day and quickly shot up the charts, leading many to predict it would be a top 5 hit by Christmas. By mid-October, though, public pushback against the song began due to some of its lyrics. For example:

American Woman, why can't you agree
God made man for Himself
But he made you for me.

Ultimately, threats of boycotts led many stations across the country to pull the song from rotation, and its climb up the charts slowed to a crawl.

In an effort to get things going again, Johnny performed the song in Nashville at a special show at Opryland. It was too little, too late, though, and the song stalled at number 23 on the charts.

According to Don, Johnny had started talking about becoming an outlaw around the same time he recorded "All American Man."

"He got to talking about wearing blue jeans and T-shirts on stage. Growing his hair longer. That kind of stuff. I told him that I might wear jeans, but they WILL have a crease in them. I think he considered "All American Man" his first outlaw song."

Steve Marple made a bold statement at the Opryland Show by coming on stage dressed in bib overalls with no shirt. That must have been a shock to the stuffed shirts that controlled things at the Grand Ole Opry.

Even as Johnny started tiptoeing down the outlaw path in his style of dress, Don said he continued to sing the same songs as before.

When he came to Greenfield on December 8 for his annual Toys For Tots show, he was dressed in his sequined uniform and showed no signs of being an outlaw. Maybe he didn't want to risk alienating his hometown fans.

Going Outlaw

1976 was a year of transition for Johnny Paycheck and, by association, the Adams Boys. Johnny's records were consistently charting in the 30s, 40s, and 50s, and booking shows became more of a chore.

In April, they went to Europe for two and a half weeks to perform shows at U.S. military bases. Gary, who didn't like to fly, stayed at home and was replaced on guitar by the Adams Boys' friend, Mike Cutright from Chillicothe, OH.

At different points over the previous few months, Johnny cut payroll by releasing vocalist Ralph May and trumpet player Dave Gray, while fiddle player Paul Justice left on his own.

Figuring that Johnny was close to shutting things down, Gary Adams and Steve Marple departed in early May, probably after a May 2 performance in Dubois, IN. I say this because on May 7 and 8, Gary and Steve played at The Mini Bar in Greenfield with their new band, the Greenfield Express.

Johnny took over lead guitar duties, and a few days later, he hired Leon Bollinger to play fiddle and Ron Stroupe to play drums. At the same time, he started calling himself Johnny Austin Paycheck and renamed the band the West Texas Music Company.

On May 10, Johnny Austin Paycheck and the West Texas Music Company arrived in Calgary, AB, for a thirteen-day engagement at Ranchman's Steakhouse. According to the May 14, 1976, edition of the *Calgary Herald*, it was here on opening night that Johnny publicly announced his new outlaw persona for the first time. He may have sung his new song, "11 Months and 29 Days", live for the first time that night as well, but I can't say that for certain.

Lacking a large outlaw-oriented catalog of songs at this point, Johnny mixed in old favorites like "She's All I Got," "Mr. Lovemaker," and "Mr. Bojangles," among others.

On May 31, Johnny filed for bankruptcy, and the bank took his bus, forcing himself and the band to travel in a van with beanbags on the floor for cots, according to Don.

Over the next few months, to save costs, Johnny and Don began performing some shows with house bands as opposed to with their own band. It was at one of these shows in Greenwich Village, NY that Don said Johnny fell off the wagon. Don recalled:

> We were in Greenwich Village at this place called The Other End. John was backstage and he kept ordering Irish Coffees from the bar. He drank two or three of them and he had whipped cream all over his beard and hands. He kept telling me he was just drinking coffee which I knew was bullshit. He wasn't shit-faced drunk, but he was getting there by the time we went on stage. After that he started drinking more and more. I don't think he was using coke yet though. He was smoking weed though. I saw the writing on the wall and started making plans to get out.

On August 7, the entire band appeared on *That Good Old Nashville Music* TV program. Johnny sang the tune from The Andy Griffith Show, "Crawdad Hole" and did quite well on it. The video is on YouTube and worth watching.

Paycheck and the Hells Angels

In the late summer of 1976, Don was backstage at the Cow Palace in San Francisco, talking with Waylon Jennings and Willie Nelson. He and Johnny were there to perform at an all-day festival featuring several country singers and some West Coast rock bands.

Johnny approached the trio excitedly and said to Don, "Come with me. I want you to meet Sonny Barger." Barger was the president of the Hells Angels Motorcycle Club and a friend of Johnny's.

Without hesitation, Don replied, "I don't want to meet that son of a bitch."

Johnny appeared unfazed and leaned in close, whispering to Don, "I think they want me to be a hitman."

"You set your expectations really high," Don commented.

This might have been the same trip when Johnny decided to rent a Learjet. According to Don, he and Johnny had performed an evening show at a club in Oxnard, California, and were scheduled to perform the next evening at a club in Malibu, just 40 miles to the south. Don said:

> We were getting ready to take a taxi down to Malibu when John says, "Don, let's take a Learjet instead."
> So, he makes a few calls, and we catch a taxi to this little airport outside of Oxnard. We take off in this Learjet, and when we land, we're in Ontario, CA, 80 miles on the other side of Malibu. We had to get a taxi to Malibu anyway. John turned a 40-mile trip into a 200-mile trip. God only knows what it cost him, and he was already broke.

Regarding the Hells Angels, Johnny became fast friends with Sonny Barger and many others. In the coming years, he would perform concerts at Hells Angels events and hang out with them at their clubhouses around the country. There is no evidence to suggest that his dream of being a hitman ever materialized.

Don said that by Labor Day, Johnny was having trouble paying the band, and he knew he had to get out, as he had a family to feed.

Based on my conversations with Don, I am almost certain that his last show was on October 2, 1976, at the Little Nashville Opry in Nashville, IN. It was my eleventh birthday.

PART FIVE

After the Spotlight

Coal Shed Publishing

Chapter 35

Gary's Time

The Greenfield Express

After leaving Johnny, Gary returned to Greenfield and formed a band that he named the Greenfield Express. The band was made up of various local musicians who, as far as I could tell, came and went from time to time. Some of the members included Steve Marple, Ralph May, Farrell Adams, and Mike Cutright, among others. The band performed throughout the area, and Gary sought financial backers to support their efforts. Despite the band's considerable talent, the project never truly gained momentum, for reasons I still don't understand."

During this period, Gary recorded a handful of records, including one in 1977 titled "Don't Break My Heart Again," which I really like. Gary's records were released on his own label, GFE Records, and distributed by Nationwide Sound of Nashville, TN.

Many of Gary's records can still be found on eBay.

Gary Adams and the Rainbow Ranch Hands

In 1978, Gary, Ralph May, and Mike Cutright got jobs playing as a house band at a club in Longview, FL called Rainbow Ranch. The band, known as Gary Adams and the Rainbow Ranch Hands, featured Gary on lead guitar, Mike on rhythm guitar, Dave Allison on bass, and Mike Milligan on drums, with Ralph as lead vocalist.

The owner of the club, Jerry Siciliano, knowing that Gary had played with Johnny Paycheck, asked him if he could arrange for Johnny to come and play a show there. Gary assured him he could, and he reached out to Johnny, who agreed to come and play.

Johnny had a plan, though. Instead of bringing his own band with him, to save on costs, he would use the house band, figuring Gary, Ralph, and Mike already knew his songs and wouldn't have trouble playing them. And since Gary's band was paid by the club, he wouldn't have to pay them either.

There was a packed house when Johnny arrived for the show. He was okay when he got there, but when he went to his dressing room, which was in a double-wide trailer that sat adjacent to the club. He immediately began ingesting a copious amount of cocaine.

As showtime approached, a large crowd was on hand, including a contingent of Hells Angels.

A line formed outside the door of Johnny's dressing room in hopes of getting his autograph, but Johnny was occupied on his hands and knees, throwing up in the toilet from all of the cocaine he had snorted.

It was nearly showtime, and Johnny was in no shape to sign autographs, so Gary and Ralph started taking items from the fans: album covers, pictures, magazines, scraps of paper, autograph books, whatever they had, and taking them inside the trailer, out of sight, where they signed Johnny's name on them and took them back out to the fans.

When the line of fans cleared out, Gary and Ralph ushered Johnny into the club and to the kitchen, where they sat him down to await his introduction.

After the band opened, Ralph introduced Johnny, and the place went crazy, led by the raucous Hells Angels.

Johnny did a couple of numbers, and as was his habit, he spent considerable time between each song tuning his guitar. In the midst of his tuning, Johnny turned to Ralph and said, "Ralph, can I get a cigarette off you?"

"Sure," Ralph said. "But how many cigarettes are you going to smoke at once?"

Johnny looked confused. "What do you mean?"

"Well, there's one clipped on to the neck of your guitar, and there's one hanging from your lips."

"Well, shit. I didn't know that," said Johnny. Then he went back to singing.

As Johnny got close to the end of his first set, several of the Hells Angels, some of them standing on chairs, began yelling, "Shove it, John! Shove it!" Meaning they wanted him to sing his recent chart-topping smash hit, "Take This Job and Shove It." Of course, John obliged them to the delight of the crowd.

Looking back on it, Ralph said, "I was really worried when John was snorting all that coke, and then the Hells Angels came riding in. I figured there would be a lot of trouble. There wasn't any though. It turned out to be a good show."

Chapter 36

Loose Ends

Don Gives Himself a Swirlie

During an interview on February 13, 2025, Don shared a humorous story with disc jockey Herb Day on his show, *Beyond The Stage*. Don recounted an incident where he washed his hair in a toilet while preparing to go on stage for a performance. He was quick to emphasize, however, that he did not brush his teeth in the toilet!

I asked Don for details during our last conversation on December 18, 2025, at his home in Greenfield.

Don recalled that in 1977 or 1978, he performed in an outdoor show in either North or South Carolina that featured Barbara Fairchild and Cajun fiddle player Doug Kershaw. The performance took place on the grounds of an old plantation house, where a trailer served as the entertainers' dressing room rather than using the facilities inside the historic home.

Don always liked to look his best onstage. So, after a long flight from Ohio, he noticed his hair wasn't looking great and wanted to wash it. He first tried using the small hand sink in the trailer, but he couldn't get his head far enough under the faucet to wet his hair properly. Since the trailer didn't have a shower, he was left with only one option: washing his hair in the toilet.

Don explained, "The commode looked clean, so I stuck my head in it and flushed. That got my hair wet, so I put the shampoo in and scrubbed my head. Then I flushed the commode a few more times to rinse."

I was laughing really hard at that point, and I said to Don, "Did you have to ask Doug Kershaw to get off the toilet so you could wash your hair?"

Don smiled, looked at my wife, and asked, "Michelle, why did you marry him?"

That made me laugh even harder. Don never lost his sense of humor.

He told me that the show was aired on television, possibly only on local channels, and that he had seen it once. However, he has never been able to find it again since then. I have also searched for it and haven't had any luck either.

Less Than Stellar Reputations

There is a quote attributed to Merle Haggard regarding the Adams Boys that some interpret as either an insult or a compliment. Haggard allegedly stated, "The Adams Boys have less-than-stellar reputations" or something similar.

It is unclear when Haggard first commented on the Adams Boys' reputations, but he reportedly mentioned it often in discussions about them. Don Adams attributed the quote to the time when Don Markham left the Paycheck band to join Merle Haggard's band. Allegedly, whenever he recounted that story, Haggard would assert that Markham had stated one reason for his departure was that the Adams Boys had "beaten the hell out of Paycheck's bus driver."

The first time Don recalled hearing about it was from country singer Lainey Hicks in the late 1970s. "I was talking to Lainey Hicks, and she said that she had been to the Waffle House the night before with a bunch of people after a show. She said that someone mentioned the Adams Boys, and someone else said that Merle Haggard told them, 'the Adams Boys have less than stellar reputations.' She said that whenever a group of musicians sat around talking about music, the Adams Boys always came up."

Don felt upset when he heard the quote repeated, saying, "Merle didn't care about our less-than-stellar reputations when he came to Ohio and needed a band to back him up. He didn't worry about our reputation when he stayed at our parents' house because he was broke."

In contrast, Gary, and especially Arnie, took great pride in Haggard's assessment of their collective reputation; they wore it like a crown.

During my research for this book, I heard that Haggard repeated the quote in the early 1970s during an on-air interview with Ralph Emery, though I have not been able to verify this.

Chapter 37

Second Run with George

No period in the Adams Boys story is more shrouded in mystery and uncertainty than their brief second collaboration with George Jones.

By the late 1970s, George was in disarray. His tumultuous marriage to Tammy Wynette ended in divorce in 1975, and his struggles with alcohol and drug abuse had escalated dramatically. Professionally, George had not recorded a number-one hit since 1974, and his habit of missing performances made promoters reluctant to book him. To make matters worse, his management team was terrible. According to George, his manager, Shug Baggot, contributed to and encouraged his cocaine addiction. He was a shadow of the man once known as "America's Number One Country Singer."

According to Gary, who shared this story on episode 351 of *The Paul Leslie Hour* podcast, which aired on January 3, 2020, George reached out to him one day and said, "Gary, I can't find anyone to work with me. I need a new band. Can you guys come down and play with me?" Gary replied that they could, and he called Don, Mike Cutright, and Steve Marple to recruit them for the band as well. At the time, Don was driving a truck and had a week left on a contract to transport grain from Greenfield to Leesburg, OH, for a local farmer. As a result, he did not join Gary, Mike, and Steve when they set off in Mike's van to meet George at his home in Florence, AL.

When they arrived at George's house in Florence, he greeted them at the door, invited them inside, and asked how much money they had. They all admitted that they were broke and barely had enough to drive to Alabama. According to the story, Gary reached into his pocket and pulled out some loose change. The exact amount varies depending on who recounts the tale, typically ranging between 27 and 74 cents. When Gary presented the change to George, he took it, added a few coins from his own pocket, and threw them out the back door into the yard to symbolize their shared financial struggles.

No one is entirely certain when these events took place. Depending on whom you ask, Don Adams, Gary Adams, Steve Marple, and Mike Cutright played with George for a period that ranged from a few weeks to a few months sometime between 1977 and 1981. I interviewed the three surviving band members: Steve, Mike, and Don (who is now deceased), and, as difficult as it is for me to understand, none could provide a precise timeline. All agreed that the collaboration occurred in the late 1970s and early 1980s, but there was no concrete information beyond that.

In his autobiography, *I Lived To Tell It All*, George made only vague remarks about the visit from Gary, Steve, and Mike to his house in Florence. He suggested that this visit occurred before he recorded "He Stopped Loving Her Today" in April 1980.

Several clues help narrow down the timeline. It's known that the Adams Boys were with George when he was admitted to Hill Crest Hospital in Birmingham, Alabama, on December 11, 1979, for drug and alcohol rehabilitation.

We also know that they were still with him when he was released on January 9, 1980. This event is well-documented on episode 2 of Mike Judge's animated show, *Tales From the Tour Bus*, as well as on *The Paul Leslie Hour* podcast.

In addition, Ron Coffey referred to it in his *Coffey Grounds* column in the January 30, 1980, edition of the *Greenfield Daily Times*. He wrote, "Speaking of musicians, I understand the Adams Boys are now called the Jones Boys. Greenfield residents Gary Adams, Don Adams, and Steve Marple, along with Chillicothe's Mike Cutright, are now on the road providing music for singer George Jones."

The March 1980 newsletter for Bobby Mackey's Music World in Wilder, KY, features an article about George Jones's performances on January 19 and 20, 1980. Notably, Cincinnati Reds catcher Johnny Bench attended the show on January 20. There is a well-known photograph of Gary Adams, George Jones, and Johnny Bench backstage at the event, as well as a lesser-known image of Gary playing guitar on stage.

During separate interviews with Don, Steve, and Mike, each mentioned specific events that occurred at shows in Texas, North Carolina, Kissimmee, FL, New York City, South Carolina, and Virginia. Using these locations, I compiled dates and venues from show bills and newspaper articles.

Ultimately, I found a newspaper article reviewing a show in El Paso, TX, on February 23, 1980, that mentions George had a "brand new band," indicating that the Adams Boys' second run with him had ended before that performance.

Evidence suggests that the Adams Boys were with George from at least November 8, 1979, to February 16, 1980. Based on Don's memory of the November 8 show in El Paso and his mention that the band played a couple of shows before he joined them, I can say with reasonable certainty that the band's first performance was on October 25, 1979, in Macon, GA. This marked George's first show since a performance on October 6 in Tulsa, OK, creating a 19-day gap that can be partly attributed to George not having a band during that time.

Therefore, for the purposes of this book, the second stint of the Adams Boys with George Jones lasted from just before October 25, 1979, to just after February 16, 1980.

Mike recounted that when he, Gary, and Steve arrived at George's home in Florence, George appeared to be in very poor condition. "He looked terrible and was so strung out on cocaine that he could hardly sing. He couldn't even remember the lyrics to his songs. Songs he had been singing for 20 years," Mike said.

George was struggling to make ends meet during this time, and the little money he did earn was being spent on cocaine and alcohol. The situation became so dire that one day, while he and the band were practicing at his home, the power company shut off his electricity because he hadn't paid his bill.

George Jones and this version of the Jones Boys, minus Don, who was still driving a truck in Ohio, likely performed their first show on October 25 at Bananas Night Club in Macon, GA. Don probably joined them for their performance on November 2 at the Nashville East Nightclub in Pennsauken, NJ.

On the following night, November 3, George did not appear for his scheduled performance at the Triple Nickel Saloon in Bear, DE.

On November 8, they performed at Chip In Danceland in Renden, TX. While they were there, the entire band fell ill (most likely from food poisoning or a stomach virus) and spent a couple of days bedridden in their hotel. According to Steve, a doctor came to the hotel to treat them, and after a day or two, they were well enough to continue their journey.

It's unclear how they were getting around the country at this time. They originally traveled in Mike's van, as George did not have a bus then. In his book, George mentioned that he had purchased a vehicle resembling a delivery truck to use until his new bus was ready. Don and Steve referred to George's new bus on several occasions, and Don shared a story about them traveling in his car. It's safe to say that, like everything else from this period, their mode of travel was varied and chaotic.

George's cocaine use was near its peak at this point, and it led to several interesting encounters, some humorous and some not. George had taken to talking in a duck voice. The duck talked like Donald Duck, and George called him "Deedoodle." George and Deedoodle would have conversations that usually turned into arguments. George referred to himself as "the old man" during these conversations.

One morning, they were getting on the bus when Deedoodle and the old man got into an argument. George would talk in his voice and then answer in the duck's voice.

Don said, "They were arguing back and forth. George was yelling, and the duck was being sarcastic, which pissed George off even more. Finally, just as the bus was pulling out, George said to the duck, 'I want your goddamned ass off this bus right now!' So, George told the bus driver to pull over and put the duck and his bags out. We hadn't gotten out of the parking lot yet, so the bus driver stopped and opened the door to let the duck off. George says, 'throw his bags out too.' So the bus driver gets off the bus, opens the baggage compartment, and sets the duck's bags on the ground."

After they finally left, George muttered that he was 'sick and tired of that son of a bitch.' However, a couple of miles down the road, George felt guilty about kicking the duck off the bus, so he had the driver turn around and pick him up

.

Don continued, "When the duck got back on the bus, George was sitting there with his arms crossed and a stern expression. He looked over his glasses at the duck and said, 'I want you to sit down and keep quiet. I don't want to hear another word out of you.' It was one of the funniest things I've ever witnessed, but it also felt a bit sad. We didn't hear from the duck again for two or three days after that."

Another time, George drew up several lines of cocaine on a tabletop and invited Steve to join him. When Steve declined the offer, George became angry, and the two exchanged words. Suddenly, George took off his glasses and threw them at Steve, hitting him in the face. This enraged Steve, and he charged at George. Don intervened, stopping him before he could reach George.

"Don't hit him, Steve," Don said, likely saving George from a beating.

Steve later remarked, "I wasn't going to let anyone get away with something like that. I didn't care if I got fired or went to jail. Don saved George's ass that day."

George was struggling with his performances at this point. Don described his behavior on stage as "unprofessional" and "clownish." Both he and Gary pleaded with George to stop using cocaine before shows, but their efforts were unsuccessful. Don recalls:

He would sing, and you couldn't even understand what he was saying. He'd forget the words and either mumble or make something up. Sometimes he'd start singing one song and switch to another halfway through. We would try to cover for him, but it was impossible to hide it. We were embarrassed to go on stage with him. Back in the '60s, he could perform while drunk, and the audience wouldn't notice. Alcohol never really affected his ability to sing. Cocaine was a different story. He was a completely different person then.

It all came to a head after a show on November 30 at the Tupperware Convention Center Auditorium in Kissimmee, FL. George had mumbled and stumbled through the show. Don remembered the confrontation on the bus afterward:

He was sitting at the front of the bus, fumbling around trying to get his cocaine laid out to snort. I just walked up to where he was sitting and knocked it out of his hand. It went on the floor, and he tried to get up, but I pushed him down in his seat. When I pushed him down, I could feel his shoulder blades poking through his jacket. I bet he didn't weigh 120 pounds. He looked up at me like he wanted to kill me.

I got right down in his face and said, "You're embarrassing yourself, and you're embarrassing us. We came down here to help you, and you're making us look stupid on stage. People are laughing at you. We're professional musicians, and if you can't act like a professional, we're going home, and you can go out there by yourself. You have to get off the cocaine."

He started crying and apologizing. He said he was done with the cocaine, and I told him he needs to get checked in somewhere to get sobered up, and then we can go back on the road and do things the right way.

After the show in Kissimmee, everyone went to George's house in Florence, where they stayed for a couple of days before heading to Tampa, FL, for a show on December 2. While they were there, George's friend Peanut Montgomery came by. Along with Don and Gary, he tried to convince George to check into a hospital to address his addiction to alcohol and drugs. However, George refused their help.

On December 2, they left for the show in Tampa. While they were gone, Montgomery obtained a court order, and George was committed against his will.

On December 11, George checked into Hill Crest Hospital in Birmingham, Alabama, for a one-month stay to recover from years of alcohol and drug abuse, with the hope of getting his career back on track.

In episode 2 of *Mike Judge Presents: Tales from the Tour Bus*, Don, Gary, and Arnie humorously recount George's intake exam at the hospital. Gary claimed that during an IQ test, George scored 62, while George stated in his autobiography that his actual score was 74.

Meanwhile, all of George's upcoming shows were canceled, including a highly anticipated appearance at the Bottom Line in New York. As a result, Don, Gary, Steve, and Mike packed up and returned to Ohio.

On New Year's Eve, Don received a call from George. "He called to thank me for helping him get treatment," Don recalled. However, George had more to say. "He said that when he got out, he wanted us to record an album together, and my name would be featured equally with his on the cover."

Unfortunately, that collaboration never came to fruition. If it had, it might have been enough to finally launch Don into stardom.

George was released from the hospital on January 9, 1980. According to his own account, he bought a six-pack of beer upon returning home and drank it while using cocaine that he had kept hidden in the house. Aside from gaining a little weight, George came out of the hospital as the same person he was when he entered.

A few days after his release, George called Don again to ask if he would take on the role of his booking agent and road manager. Don declined the offer since he lacked experience in booking shows and didn't believe he would do a good job. However, he did contact Bobby Mackey, who owned Bobby Mackey's Music World in Wilder, KY, and managed to get George booked for two nights on January 19 and 20. This would be George's first performance on stage since completing rehab.

It was about this time that George started talking about a song that he was considering recording. He told the band, "This song is gonna bring us out of it and put us back on top. It's kind of morbid, though."

He played the song for them, and although they agreed it was morbid, they all encouraged George to record it.

"I knew it was a good song," Don recalled later. "It was morbid, but I thought people would like it. It was different from anything else being recorded at the time. Plus, what did he have to lose at that point?"

The song is titled "He Stopped Loving Her Today." It marked George Jones' return to the forefront of country music and is widely regarded as one of the greatest country songs ever recorded.

The Adams Boys would not benefit from it, though. Similar to Johnny Paycheck's "Take This Job and Shove It," Don and Gary would miss out again.

The situation began to deteriorate almost right after the shows at Bobby Mackey's Music World. George found himself back in the same place he had been before going to rehab. The influence of whiskey and cocaine continued to impact his behavior, ultimately harming both his career and his health.

After a show in China Grove, NC, on January 25, Don, Gary, Steve, and Mike got into either Mike's van or Don's car (it's not entirely clear which) and prepared to drive to Ohio for a few days off before hitting the road again. A young woman followed the band outside and began talking to them. Don and Gary had gone back inside the club for some reason, and when they returned, they found the woman had climbed into the passenger seat of the car. Seeing her, Don told her they were leaving and asked her to get out of the car.

The woman got out of the car and then climbed into the back seat, where Steve and Mike were sitting. They told her to get out of the car, but she refused, insisting she wanted to hang out for a while. Don informed her that they were leaving, and unless she wanted to go to Ohio, she better get out. Once again, the woman refused, so Don started the car and drove away.

Don explained, "She wouldn't get out of the car, so I took off with her in it. I got out on the interstate and drove about 30 miles before I pulled off on an exit and parked the car in a motel parking lot. I got out of the car, opened the back door, took her by the wrist, and pulled her out of the car. I said this was the end of the line and handed her a twenty-dollar bill. I told her that ought to get her a taxi home. Then I took off, headed north."

Sometime around February 10, everyone met in Nashville to go on tour again. George had his new bus then, and their first trip was across the country to California, where they performed for two nights at the famous Palomino Club in North Hollywood. Leaving California, they immediately drove back east and started a run of shows in Virginia and the Carolinas. Whoever drew up that itinerary clearly wasn't thinking or didn't have a basic knowledge of geography.

George was drinking heavily and using cocaine liberally again, so things had been pretty tense. On February 16, at a show in Danville, VA, at a club called the Wishbone, everything came to a head. Towards the end of the show, George forgot the words to his song, so Gary went into a guitar break trying to help George get back on track.

George realized what was going on and, instead of trying to recover, he turned around and grabbed the neck of Gary's guitar. Gary stopped playing, and George said, "Gary, what am I paying you for, to play guitar or to cover me up?"

Steve saw it all. "Gary was pissed. He didn't want anyone touching his guitar. His face turned red with anger, and probably embarrassment, too. Gary turned the volume up on his guitar and said, 'You play the motherfucker then.' Then he dropped it on the stage and walked off. When he dropped that guitar, the sound about busted everyone's eardrums."

They finished the show without Gary or his guitar.

After the show, the band loaded up on the bus for the return trip to Nashville while George either flew home or went with someone in their car. George's gear, however, including his antique Martin acoustic guitar, was loaded on the bus.

When the bus arrived in Nashville, everyone except for Steve loaded their gear into Mike's van for the return trip to Greenfield. Steve left his drums on the bus because they were too cumbersome to transport, and he figured they would be back on the bus next week anyway.

Mike dropped off Don, Gary, and Steve in Greenfield before driving home to Chillicothe. While he was unpacking his gear, he noticed George's guitar was still in the van. Assuming it had been accidentally loaded into his van when they transferred their equipment from the bus, he decided to leave it there for the time being. He planned to return it to George the following week.

A day or two later, Gary went to Mike's house, and when he left, he took George's guitar with him. It appears that Gary, likely retaliating for George's behavior on stage at the Wishbone, had confiscated the guitar with the intention of selling it. He followed through on that plan when a friend of his purchased it. It is unclear whether the buyer was aware that the guitar was stolen or how much he paid Gary for it.

Author's Note: *In the following few paragraphs, I will refer to George Jones, George Richey, and Paul Richey by their full names, except when someone is speaking, as indicated by parentheses. Doing so will help readers differentiate between individuals with the same names, such as George Jones and George Richey, and George Richey and Paul Richey.*

A few days after returning to Greenfield, Don received a call at home from George Richey, Tammy Wynette's manager and husband. George Richey was the brother of Paul Richey, who was George Jones' manager at the time. During the call, George Richey informed Don that he, Gary, Steve, and Mike were fired because they were considered a bad influence on George Jones.

It's unclear why George Richey, rather than Paul Richey, reached out to Don. It's possible that Paul Richey made the call, and Don mixed up the names. I asked Don multiple times whether he was certain it was George Richey who made the decision to fire them, and he always insisted it was.

It was widely known by that time that George Jones and Tammy Wynette were reuniting. This time strictly as a duet, rather than as a romantic couple. Therefore, it's likely the Richeys considered themselves co-managers of both George Jones and Tammy.

Don said the idea that they were a bad influence on George Jones was ridiculous. When Don told Gary, Gary said that waking up in the morning was a bad influence on George Jones.

In reality, Don thought they were fired for a combination of reasons: the Adams Boys were difficult to control, the Richeys wanted a band that was a little more malleable, and George Jones was broke; another band could be put together for a lot less money.

During one of our interviews, Don shared with me a thought he had kept to himself for years regarding their firing. He speculated that there may have been another reason behind it. He believed that the young woman who had refused to get out of their car in North Carolina might have alleged to someone that she had been assaulted by members of George Jones band. He thought that this accusation could have eventually reached George Jones and his management team. Don made it clear that no one had ever discussed this with him; he just always considered it a possibility.

"First of all, that girl was not assaulted," Don insisted. "No one laid a hand on her except me when I pulled her from the car. If she told someone that, though, it would make sense that George would want to distance himself from us so it didn't interfere with his reunion with Tammy or with his release of 'He Stopped Loving Her Today,' which everyone thought could be a hit."

That does make some sense. Certainly more sense than saying the Adams Boys were a bad influence on George Jones.

The story didn't stop there. While all of this was happening, Ralph May was in Nashville and met with Paul Richey in his office regarding another matter. While there, Ralph noticed that Steve's drums were sitting in a hallway. Curious, Ralph inquired about it. "Why are Steve Marple's drums sitting in the hallway?" Ralph asked.

"Someone stole George's guitar, and I'm holding them for ransom until we get it back," Paul Richey answered.

"You don't think Steve stole it, do you? I know Steve really well, and that doesn't sound like something he would do," Ralph said.

"I don't know who stole it," Paul Richey said. "But I'm going to hold onto these drums until we get them back."

When Ralph got back to Greenfield, he told Don what he had seen.

According to Don, when he found out that Ralph had seen Steve's drums in Paul Richey's Nashville office, he wasn't aware that someone had stolen George Jones' guitar. When he asked the other guys about it, Gary, after a little prodding, told Don that he had taken it and sold it. Regardless, Don was determined to get Steve's drums back, so he formulated a pl an.

Don's plan was simple. He would round up a posse, drive to Nashville, and secure Steve's drums. So, the very next day, Don, Ralph, Gary, and Steve drove to Nashville.

According to Don, when they arrived in Nashville, he drove straight to George Richey's office and knocked on his door. George Richey answered the door, surprised to see Don, Ralph, Gary, and Steve standing before him.

"Why are you here?" George Richey asked

"We're here to get Steve's drums," Don shot back.

"I'm keeping them until we get George's guitar back," George Richey said.

"I don't know anything about a guitar," Don said. "But you have two choices: You can give us back Steve's drums, or I can whip your ass, and then you can give us back Steve's drums. Either way, we're taking the drums."

Sensing that Don was serious and realizing he was out-numbered 4 to 1, George Richey retrieved the drums, and Don and his posse left the premises.

Don added that the group spent the night in Nashville and stopped by a couple of clubs to listen to music and visit with friends before returning to Greenfield the next morning.

I interviewed Don and Ralph together about the issue, and Don stated that this is how it was resolved. It's important to note again that, when telling this story, Don consistently referred to George Richey rather than Paul Richey. As I mentioned earlier, I believe Don was confusing the Richey brothers, but he was adamant that he was correct. He recounted this story several times, and it never changed; he always maintained it was George Richey and never mentioned Paul Richey.

Additionally, Ralph later confided in me that he wasn't part of Don's group and was unaware of the trip to Nashville. However, he noted that Don, Gary, and Steve could have gone, but he simply didn't know about it.

Steve remembered the episode differently. He couldn't remember exactly how he found out that his drums were being held, but said it might have been Don who told him. "Somehow," Steve said, "a friend of Gary's from Columbus***, found out about what was going on. Gary must have told him, and he knew who had bought the guitar. So he bought it back and called down to Nashville and told them to send my drums up to Ohio, and he would see that the guitar was returned."

According to Steve, Paul Richey, satisfied with the arrangement, shipped his drums to Cincinnati on a Greyhound bus.

"They shipped my drums to Cincinnati on a bus, and me and Faye (Steve's wife) drove down there to the Greyhound bus station and picked them up. The cases were beat to hell, but the drums were okay."

Steve was very grateful to Gary's friend for interceding. "He didn't have to do that," Steve said. "He bought that guitar back with his own money and wouldn't accept any money for doing it. He really helped me out." (Gary's friend will remain anonymous)

This episode about Steve's drums illustrates how people can remember events differently. It serves as a perfect example of how stories evolve into myths and myths into legends.

Chapter 38

Odds and Ends

Over the course of my fourteen months of research for this book, I have heard many stories. I've included most of the bigger stories, placing them in the proper context within the main body of the book. Meaning that I have placed them in a sequence that makes it easy for you, the reader, to understand.There are other stories that, though they may not add significantly to the overall story, are still interesting and worth reading. Many of these stories lack specifics such as names, locations, or time periods. I believe they are true, or at least mostly true, because the people who told me the stories were either directly involved or had heard them from people who were.

Anyway, feel free to use these in polite conversation, or anytime you experience uncomfortable silence in a crowded room.

    • One time in a Texas dance hall, presumably in the

1960s, during a break between sets, Don Adams was approached by an intoxicated man who was upset that his wife had said that Don had "a nice ass." In true Adams Boys fashion, Don punched the man in the face, leaving him sprawled on the floor. Don then told the bouncer that the man had swung at him, prompting the bouncer to throw the man out. Don explained that he punched the person because he sensed trouble and wanted to get it over with.

- According to Diane McCall, there was an incident involving Gary Adams and Buddy Emmons, perhaps in Las Vegas in the early 1970s. Buddy was in bed with a woman in his hotel room when Gary stopped by to use the bathroom. (Did Gary have a key to the room?) After Gary left, either Buddy or his lady friend went to use the bathroom, only to discover that Gary had pooped in the sink. Another person, who wanted to remain anonymous, told me that Gary did the same thing at a Merle Haggard show sometime in the early 80s. Apparently, Gary had been backstage hanging out before the show, and when Haggard and his band, the Strangers, took the stage to perform, he pooped in the sink in the Strangers' dressing room. My wife was appalled by these stories and asked me if I would have ever done such a thing. I assured her that I would not, but in my younger days, I would have encouraged someone else to do it and would have laughed with my mouth wide open when they did.

- Three Adams brothers, Don, Farrell, and Darrell, told me that sometime around 1965, Gary accidentally shot himself in the leg while practicing his quick-draw technique at his parents' house in Greenfield.

I couldn't find any information in the newspapers about it, but I 100% believe it happened.

- Legend has it that George Jones bought a house in Greenfield in the 1960s to stay in whenever he was in town. I've heard it my whole life. According to Don, it isn't true, "George only came to Greenfield a handful of times and only spent the night here once or twice, at Paul Angel's house. No one in Greenfield knew George Jones better than I did. If he had a house here, I would have known about it."

Every Time Two Fools Collide 1977

In 1977, Don recorded a demo of a song that ultimately reached Number 1 on the Billboard Country Chart. The song was "Every Time Two Fools Collide."

According to Don, the demo was being shopped around to record producers in Nashville in hopes of securing him a new record deal that would allow him to release the song.

It wasn't to be, though. Someone took Don's demo to Kenny Rogers, who ended up recording it with Dottie West. The duet topped the charts with it, and that was that.

"I understand why they gave it to Kenny," said Don. "I mean, he was already a star. You could have a Kenny Rogers record or a Don Adams record. I understand their choice."

With all due respect to Kenny Rogers and Dottie West, Don's version of "Every Time Two Fools Collide" is the definitive version. Listen for yourself, and I think you will agree.

Barbara Fairchild

In 1977, Gary, along with Mike Cutright, joined Barbara Fairchild's band for a 10-date coast-to-coast tour. The tour included a benefit show in Barbara's hometown of Paragould, AR, on November 14 at the Knoble High School Auditorium. On December 7, the band played in Wichita Falls, TX, at the Fedmart Building, where the heat went out just before the show started. By the end of the night, the temperature inside had dropped to about 40 degrees.

At the end of the tour, Barbara played a show at Possum Holler in Washington Court House, OH, and she gave the proceeds to the band to split for Christmas. Before the show, Barbara and the band, along with several guests from Greenfield, gathered at Gary's house for dinner.

*Mural in downtown Greenfield, Ohio,
January 19, 2026, photo by Eric Grate*

Marty Robbins

In 1982, Marty Robbins was looking for a guitar player. Unbeknownst to the other, Gary and Mike Cutright both applied for the job, and both went separately to Nashville to meet with Robbins. Robbins liked both equally, so he hired them.

After he was hired, Gary played several demos of songs he had written for Robbins. Robbins liked almost all of them and wanted to record several. The one he recorded on the album he was working on at the time was called "Baby That's Love." That song was written by Gary and Don, and Don had recorded it on his 1975 album under the title "That's Love."

Gary and Mike toured with Robbins for about six months and played with him on what turned out to be Marty's last show, on November 30, 1982, at the Cincinnati Convention Center in Cincinnati, OH.

Robbins had a massive heart attack on December 2, 1982, and died on December 8.

This is where things get really interesting. Back in March 1963, Gary was on stage with Patsy Cline at her last concert. Fast forward to 1982, and Gary was on stage with Marty Robbins at his last concert. Gary Adams is the only person on earth who can say that he played with Patsy Cline and Marty Robbins, two country music legends, at their last shows. Wow your friends with that at the next party.

Chapter 39

The Final Years

The Quiet Years

By the mid-1980s, the Adams Boys had largely retired from the serious pursuit of country music. All three were in their mid-40s to early 50s by then and working regular jobs like driving a truck, selling cars, laying carpet, doing warranty work on mobile homes, and working as a prison guard, among others.

Arnie had stepped away from the road earlier, in the early 1970s, with eight kids to raise. That was hard to do from a tour bus halfway across the country.

Don and Gary continued to perform in local bands, and you were apt to see them at nearly every local festival, fair, and benefit show within 50 miles of Greenfield. Don made it clear that by that time, he was more interested in watching his daughters' ball games than playing music, and he made sure his schedule allowed for it.

That's not to say nothing noteworthy happened.

On June 7, 1991, a benefit concert was held at the Paxton Theatre in Bainbridge for Cathy Clouser Adams, wife of Farrell Adams. Cathy suffered from ALS, also known as Lou Gehrig's disease. Headlining the show was Greenfield's Ralph May. Also featured were Farrell Adams, Don Adams, Darrell Adams, Gary Adams, Richard Martin, Mike Cutright, Dave Harden, Steve Marple, Faye Marple, Greg Smith, Roger Cooper, Chuck Anderson, Jim Bristley, Marcie Howland, Brenda Harden, and Kimberly Carter.

That same year, Gary opened a recording studio in Greenfield called Greenfield Express Recording. It was outfitted with state-of-the-art equipment, and Gary also gave guitar and vocal lessons there.

On Saturday, May 2, 1992, the McClain High School Athletic Boosters put on a country music extravaganza at the McClain High School Auditorium in Greenfield. The show, dubbed "The Gathering," featured a who's who of area talent including Don Adams, Darrell Adams, Ralph May, Steve Marple, Dave and Brenda Harden, Chuck Anderson, Rod West, and Mike Cutright.

Gary's Accident

On March 6, 2004, Gary was involved in a severe automobile accident on the way home from a show in eastern Ohio. Gary and Jim Bristley were hit by two separate cars. Gary was severely injured, suffering broken bones in his left arm and hand, a broken neck, and numerous internal injuries. Unfortunately, neither Gary nor the drivers of the two vehicles that struck him had insurance.

Don went to work organizing a benefit show for Gary, which was held on June 20, 2004, at the Colony Theatre in Hillsboro, Ohio. Headlining the show were Darrell McCall and Buddy Emmons. Also appearing were Nashville musicians Doug Jernigan, Greg Galbraith, and David Smith, along with Bobby Mackey, Don Adams, Darrell Adams, Faye Marple, Dee Penn, Ralph May, Mike Cutright, Dave Short, Joe Adams, Red Jenkins, Steve Moore, Steve Marple, and De an Enboden.

A funny moment occurred during the night's festivities when Gary, who was being wheeled to the stage in a wheelchair by Ralph May, turned to Ralph and said, "Hey Ralph, when we get down close to the stage, I'm going to fall out of the wheelchair onto the floor."

"Why would you want to do that?" Ralph asked.

"It ought to be worth an extra two or three thousand dollars," Gary responded.

Both had a good laugh.

A Last Hurrah

On July 16, 2016, a big country concert was put on in downtown Greenfield during the Greene Countrie Town Festival. The lineup featured the Adams Boys, Gary, Don, and Darrell, along with Steve Marple on drums, Dean Bowden on guitar, Doug Jernigan on steel guitar, Eli Bishop on fiddle, and Billy Dingus on piano. The ensemble was collectively known as the Adams Brothers and the Greenfield Express. Gary unofficially dubbed the show *The Last Roundup*.

In 2017, Mike Judge, creator of *Beavis and Butt-head* and *King of the Hill*, produced a show called *Mike Judge Presents: Tales from the Tour Bus*, a twelve-episode series highlighting stories of famous country music stars. Episode one was about Johnny Paycheck and featured the Adams Boys prominently. Episode two was about George Jones and once again featured the Adams Boys.

When I spoke to Don about his experience making *Tales from the Tour Bus*, he had mixed feelings. He was happy to get the exposure, as a whole new generation of fans got to learn about the Adams Boys. On the flip side, he wasn't happy with the pay or amenities, which were less than what he would have expected.

The brainchild behind *Tales from the Tour Bus* was none other than Greenfield's own Jeff Cropper. Jeff had the idea for the show and was somehow able to get the attention of Mike Judge, who liked the concept and made it happen.

If you haven't seen episodes one and two of *Mike Judge Presents: Tales from the Tour Bus*, I sincerely encourage you to watch them. They are incredibly hilarious.

Shortly after the Mike Judge show aired, the Adams brothers, Don, Gary, and Darrell, produced a CD called *The Last Bandstanding*. Each brother contributed five songs to it. It's a great collection, and if you can get your hands on a copy, you'll be sure to enjoy it.

Recognition

On August 21, 2022, Don, Arnie, and Gary were inducted into the Ohio Country Music Hall of Fame, along with Johnny Paycheck, at the Keeping It Country Farm Music Venue near Waynesville. Gary and Johnny were honored posthumously as Johnny had died at age 64 in 2003 from emphysema and asthma, and Gary passed on January 7, 2022, at the Greenfield Area Medical Center following a bout with COVID. The awards were presented by country music DJ Herb Day.

During his acceptance speech, Arnie gave credit to Johnny Paycheck, saying, "We all three owe whatever we had gained to Johnny Paycheck because he left here on his own and went to Nashville, and he had the talent to back it up."

On February 19, 2023, the Adams Boys, Don, Arnie, and Gary, were awarded the prestigious Founders of the Sound Award at the 2023 Ameripolitan Music Awards, held at the Guest House at Graceland in Memphis, Tennessee. Gary was honored posthumously. When presented with their awards, the Adams Boys received a standing ovation from an enthusiastic crowd thrilled to meet and talk with the two country l egends.

Paul Angel

No one did more for country music in Greenfield than Paul Angel.

Paul Angel "Dunk" at his Club 28, in Greenfield, OH Circa: Late 1950s

I'm sorry to say I don't know many details about Paul's life. I do know that his family came to Greenfield from Rarden, Ohio, when Paul was very young. At some point, probably very early on, Paul fell in love with country music. He learned to play guitar, and although he never pursued it much past a hobby, he became very good at it. Good enough that he quickly earned a reputation as a teacher. You can almost bet that between the late 1940s and mid-1980s, nearly every guitar player from Greenfield who took it seriously owed some form of gratitude to Paul Angel.

Paul opened a nightclub called Club 28 on West Jefferson Street in Greenfield sometime in the 1950s. Johnny Paycheck, then known as Donnie Lytle, was said to have played at Club 28 on several occasions when he was just a teenager. Club 28's jukebox was full of pure country classics, and you could get six plays for a quarter.

Club 28 Greenfield, OH Circa: Mid to Late 1950s Courtesy of Randy Angel

Paul and his wife, Donna, were known to invite local musicians to their house for all-night jam sessions in their living room. Paul invested in instruments and recording equipment until the house became so full that he had a basement dug under it. According to his son Randy, Paul paid a man one dollar an hour to dig the basement by hand with a pickaxe, a shovel, and a wheelbarrow. When the basement was done, Paul filled it with high-tech recording equipment and started recording the jam sessions that went on there.

Donnie Lytle, by that time known as Donny Young, was a frequent visitor, along with his good friend Darrell Mc-

Call. Soon the Adams brothers joined in too, first Gary, then Don and finally Arnie. Through Donny's contacts, some of Nashville's biggest stars started dropping by, including Buck Owens, Don Rich, and George Jones. In 1966, a young Merle Haggard came to Greenfield and recorded in Paul's basement. Other young artists joined in as well, including Ralph May, Farrell Adams, Darrell Adams, Richard Martin, and many others.

Donny Young became Johnny Paycheck in the mid-1960s, and by 1971 he was a major country music star. That didn't keep him from Greenfield, though. Whenever Johnny came back, he was at Paul Angel's house. He'd bring along his band, The Cashiers, and they'd use Paul's basement for rehearsals for big shows in the area.

I once asked Randy Angel if his dad taught Johnny Paycheck to play guitar. Randy said, "I don't know that he taught him to play guitar, but he did teach him to play it the right way."

Paul was a huge supporter of Johnny Paycheck, and he started a small museum in his home dedicated to Johnny's career.

Don Adams once told me, "Without Johnny Paycheck, there would have been no Adams Boys. And without Paul Angel, Johnny Paycheck would have never left Greenfield."

I'll say it again: no one did more for country music in Greenfield than Paul Angel.

Paul died on November 14, 1996, at 78 years old, and Greenfield lost a treasure.

When Greenfield's Mount Rushmore of country music is erected, five individuals belong at the top: Johnny Paycheck, Don Adams, Gary Adams, Arnie Adams, and Paul Angel.

Saying Goodbye

Sadly, Arnie passed after a long battle with cancer on August 28, 2023.

Don was afforded one final honor on June 8, 2025, when he rode as grand marshal in the parade at the Greenfield Music Festival in Greenfield, Ohio. I'm proud to say that as he rode by, I stood at the curb waving at him, and he pointed at me, smiled, and mouthed, "Thank you."

Don passed on February 1, 2026, at his home in Greenfield after a long, courageous battle with cancer.

A Personal Note

I had the privilege of spending eleven and a half months as Don Adams' friend. It was an experience I'll never forget, one I'll cherish for the rest of my life.

Don was an incredible man, and not just because of his voice. Don impressed me as he fought cancer the entire time we spent together. He never felt sorry for himself, and I never heard him complain. He always had a smile and could always crack a joke. He spent much more time talking about his children and grandchildren than he did about his cancer.

I met with Don in his home nearly twenty times and spoke with him on the phone two or three times a month. The only time I think I was bothering him was when a Cincinnati Reds ball game was on. He answered every question I asked, including some I don't think he wanted to answer. I found him honest and forthcoming, even when it came to critiquing himself.

The first time I sat down to talk with him, in February of 2025, I asked what had kept him from reaching superstardom in country music.

"I didn't have the fire in my belly," Don said. "It just wasn't that important to me. Not nearly as important as my family at home."

Could you have made it if you really wanted to?

"Who knows? I think I was good enough, but that's not always all it takes. You have to want it. John wanted it. Gary wanted it to an extent, but he was kind of like me. He loved his family, although he wasn't very good at showing it at times. I guess maybe I wasn't either."

What would it have looked like had you had fire in your belly?

"It would have meant uprooting my kids, my wife, and moving them to Nashville, even though I knew my wife didn't want to go. Honestly, I wasn't crazy about taking my kids down there either."

Don Adams, thank you for sharing your story with me. Thank you for being a great example. Most of all, thank you for being my friend.

PART SIX

Shoot Out at the North High Lounge

Coal Shed Publishing

Chapter 40

Details

Author's Note: On December 19, 1985, Johnny Paycheck shot Larry Wise inside the North High Lounge in Hillsboro, Ohio. That is a documented fact. However, the official account of the events leading up to the shooting is questionable, and the public's perception, forty years later, of what occurred inside the bar is influenced as much by legend as it is by fact.

The original manuscript of this book included a brief mention of what happened that night, but it was only a few paragraphs within another chapter. After all, this book is not about Johnny Paycheck; it's about the Adams Boys. Initially, I felt that the details did not significantly contribute to their story. However, as I conducted more research, I uncovered numerous inconsistencies, unanswered questions, and direct connections to the Adams Boys. Consequently, I decided to dedicate an entire chapter to this important event. While it is a part of their story, the Adams Boys take on supporting roles rather than starring ones.

Chapter 41

The Legend

On December 19, 1985, Johnny Paycheck was hanging out at a Hells Angels clubhouse somewhere in Maryland. The clubhouse was under FBI surveillance, and the FBI may have tipped off the Hells Angels that a rival club planned to blow it up.

Learning that something was up, Johnny and the Hells Angels left in a hurry, but Johnny ran back inside and grabbed a large stash of Peruvian cocaine and two suitcases full of an undetermined amount of cash. He then got back in his car and took off on the seven-hour drive to Greenfield to visit his mother for Christmas.

After visiting his mother in Greenfield, Johnny drove 17 miles to Hillsboro. Once in Hillsboro, he stopped at the North High Lounge, a bar located near the center of town. There, he met two men, Larry Wise and Lloyd Bowers, both from Greenfield. Recognizing Johnny, Wise and Bowers initiated a conversation with him, and Johnny treated them to a beer.

After chatting amicably for a short while, Johnny, under the influence of copious amounts of cocaine and whiskey, became offended at the mention of turtle soup. In a fit of anger, he drew a .22 caliber revolver from the waistband of his pants and shot Wise in the head. Paycheck then ran from the bar, got into his car, and sped away.

Johnny fled to the house of Larry "Red Dog" Adams in nearby Sabina, where he was arrested a few hours later.

Johnny was found guilty at trial and sentenced to nine years in prison at the Chillicothe Correctional Institute, where he performed a concert with Merle Haggard.

After serving two years, Ohio Governor Richard Celeste commuted Johnny's sentence and released him from prison. The rest is history. Or is it? After all, no one, including Johnny Paycheck, has ever disputed the fact that Johnny committed the act that he was ultimately convicted of. There is more to the story, though, and upon closer examination, certain pieces of the legend surrounding the event fail to fit the puzzle.

In the following pages, I will use eyewitness testimony, media accounts, and one-on-one interviews with people tied to the event to dissect the legend and present a more accurate picture of what really happened.

Chapter 42

The Facts?

The facts of the case, at least as established at trial, are that on December 18, 1985, Johnny Paycheck drove from Nashville, not Maryland, to his hometown of Greenfield, Ohio, to spend Christmas with his mother and visit his friend Paul Angel, who was recovering from a heart attack. On that same day, Johnny drove to neighboring Sabina, Ohio, to see his longtime friend, Larry "Red Dog" Adams. In fact, Johnny planned to stay at Red Dog's house during his visit home because he thought that his mother's house in Greenfield was too small.

The following day, December 19, Johnny visited several friends, including Red Dog, and decided to go out to relax at the North High Lounge in nearby Hillsboro, Ohio.

Johnny arrived at the North High Lounge around 10:00 PM on December 19. Upon entering, he recognized a man named Dick McCormick and sat beside him at the bar before ordering a drink.

A short time later, a man from Greenfield named Lloyd Bowers recognized Johnny. So Bowers approached him and struck up a conversation. Despite both men being from Greenfield, they did not know one another. After speaking amicably for a few minutes, Bowers' friend, Larry Wise, joined the conversation briefly, and Johnny bought Bowers and Wise a drink. Wise then left and went to another part of the bar. While chatting, Johnny became angry when Bowers made mention of his (Johnny's) family, specifically his brothers. In an attempt to diffuse the situation, Bowers suggested to Johnny that the two exchange their hats. After the exchange, both men calmed down and resumed a cordial conversation.

A few moments later, Wise joined Johnny and Bowers at the bar, where another argument erupted over a perceived insult regarding turtle soup.

The argument concluded when Johnny drew a pistol and shot Wise in the head.

After falling to the floor, Wise got back on his feet and ran from the bar.

Johnny picked up Wise's hat from the floor before running out of the bar. He got into his car and drove back to Red Dog's house in Sabina, which is 31 miles north of Hillsboro.

An all-points bulletin was issued for Johnny, and he was arrested at Red Dog's house in the early morning hours of December 20. Johnny was charged with felonious assault, later reduced to aggravated assault, and he was incarcerated at the Highland County Jail in Hillsboro.

According to the December 27 edition of the *Greenfield Daily Times*, a preliminary hearing took place that day in Hillsboro Municipal Court before Judge Jon Hapner.

During the hearing, Larry Wise, the victim, testified that Johnny and Lloyd Bowers were conversing and exchanging hats when he approached Johnny and asked if he had a place to stay, and stated, "I know how it is when you're playing music." Wise further testified that people were shaking Johnny's hand, patting him on the back, and playing his music. "Everyone was getting along just fine," he stated.

At some point, the conversation turned to wildlife, and Wise mentioned that Bowers asked Johnny if he had ever eaten deer or turtle meat. Johnny responded, "Do you take me for some kind of country hick?" At that moment, Johnny drew a gun, pointed it at Wise, and fired, knocking Wise's hat off and grazing his head. Fearing for his life, Wise ran from the bar, while Johnny ran to his car and fled.

Ernest Turner, the owner of the North High Lounge, testified that Johnny and Bowers had a brief argument before Bowers walked away. He stated that Bowers approached Johnny again, and they argued once more. At that point, bartender Paul "Zero" Johnson informed Turner that Johnny had a gun. Turner then ran around the bar towards Johnny and Bowers, just as Johnny shot Wise, noting, "I think Wise had stepped between Paycheck and Bowers." Turner also testified that he did not see the actual shooting take place.

Judge Hapner found probable cause and bound Johnny over to the Grand Jury. Johnny was returned to the Highland County Jail until he was released a few days later after posting his $25,000 cash bond, thus allowing him to continue touring and playing scheduled shows.

One of those shows was on New Year's Eve at the Sunnyside Inn in Allensburg, OH, near Hillsboro. During the show, Johnny stood on the stage and said, "I guess you're all wondering why I shot that guy. Because he needed it." This incident would come up later at trial.

On January 3, 1986, a Highland County Grand Jury indicted Johnny on charges of felonious assault, carrying a concealed weapon, and tampering with evidence.

The tampering with evidence charge stemmed from Johnny's admission that he threw the gun he shot Wise with out of the window of his car somewhere between Hillsboro and Sabina. Johnny told police that he didn't know exactly where he was when he disposed of the weapon because he got lost on the way to Sabina and took several wrong turns before recognizing a familiar road that finally led him to Red Dog's house.

In what was perhaps an effort to convince Prosecutor Coss to drop the tampering charge, the defense hired Jim Wilson, a former Greenfield police officer and investigator, to find the gun. Johnny told Wilson he thought he had thrown it into a creek while crossing a bridge. That information helped Wilson narrow his search, and he located the weapon more than two weeks after the shooting, in a creek on top of ice on Ohio Route 72 in Clinton County, just past the Highland County line.

On May 12, 1986, Johnny Paycheck filed a lawsuit against the North High Lounge and its owner, Ernest Turner. In the suit, Johnny claimed that Turner failed to ensure his safety by not removing intoxicated patrons who were posing a threat to him. He alleged that he suffered from "fright and extreme emotional distress" and that he became involved in a life-threatening situation, which left him "emotionally scarred and economically devastated." The lawsuit sought $3 million in compensatory damages and an additional $3 million in punitive damages.

The following day, May 13, Johnny's trial began in Highland County Municipal Court with Judge Darrel Hottle presiding.

The prosecution began by calling its witnesses.

According to an article in the *Greenfield Daily Times* from May 14, 1986, Ernest Turner, the owner of North High Lounge, testified that there were only five people present in his bar on the night of the shooting. He stated that neither Johnny, Larry Wise, nor Lloyd Bowers appeared to be visibly intoxicated. Turner also testified that there were two arguments among the three men, with the second argument escalating into the shooting.

Turner testified that he did not witness the shooting as he was running from behind the bar towards Johnny after bartender Paul "Zero" Johnson informed him that Johnny had a gun. Turner said that he approached Johnny from behind after the shooting, grabbed his shoulders, and pushed him against the jukebox. While still under oath, Turner stated that Johnny then turned, pointed the gun at Turner's stomach, and asked, "Why are you pushing me?" Turner responded by telling Johnny he should leave. At that point, Johnny tucked the gun into his waistband and ran out the door.

Johnson, the bartender, took the stand and testified that he initially served Johnny "a shot of whiskey with a Michelob chaser." Later, Johnny switched to "Grandad," presumably Old Grandad bourbon, and had two double shots. Johnson also mentioned that Wise and Bowers were drinking Miller beer, though he did not specify whether it was Miller High Life, known as the "Champagne of Beers," or Miller Lite, a lower-calorie, less filling beer.

Continuing with his testimony, Johnson said he heard Johnny say, "What do you think, I'm a hick?" before pulling a long-barreled small-caliber gun with what looked like pearl handles from his waistband, and shooting Wise in the head.

Johnson went on to say that Johnny was acting "hyper" that night and that he didn't hear Wise or Bowers make any threats towards Johnny.

After the shooting occurred, Johnson said that Wise ran out the door, and Johnny yelled, "Come back! I didn't mean to do it!"

Lloyd Bowers took the witness stand and, according to newspaper reports, testified that on the night of the shooting, the conversation began amicably. However, at some point, someone mentioned deer meat and turtle soup, which angered Johnny and led him to shoot Wise. Bowers stated that Johnny said, "I'm outta here," then walked out the door, got into his car, and sped away.

One of the most revealing and lesser-known testimonies came from a man named Al Staten, who was identified as the former owner of the Coffee Cup Restaurant in Hillsboro. On the night of the shooting, Staten happened to be standing along North High Street directly across from the North High Lounge

As reported in the *Greenfield Daily Times*, Staten said, "I was standing in the doorway of Miller's (clothing store), waiting for a ride home. Some guy (Larry Wise) ran out (of the North High Lounge) and hid behind a car. He squatted down. And (Paycheck) came out and yelled at this guy in a crabby-like voice, and (Wise) hollered back, and then (Wise) ran up the street... (Paycheck) got in the car... he had something in his hand. He backed out of there like he was going to a fire. He didn't turn the lights on until he got through the intersection."

In an unusual move, Johnny's attorney, Ralph Buss, subpoenaed former Ohio Governor James Rhodes to testify on behalf of the defense. His reasoning was that Johnny had received an award in 1978, presented by then-Governor Rhodes. Governor Rhodes was simply the presenter and had no hand in Johnny's selection for receiving the award. Rhodes testified on the second day of the trial, but his testimony was kept from the jury and did nothing to exonerate Johnny.

Jim Wilson, the man hired by the defense to find the gun used in the shooting, testified that after finding the gun, he discussed it with Johnny's original attorney, William Peele, then contacted the Hillsboro Police Department (HPD). Wilson said he made several attempts to turn the gun over to HPD but there seemed to be little interest on their part in picking up the gun. Finally, the Hillsboro Police Chief himself came to Wilson's Greenfield residence to retrieve it.

Johnny's road manager, John Long, testified in Johnny's defense. Long said it was he who gave Johnny the .22 caliber single-action Ruger revolver used in the shooting. He was worried that Johnny was making the trip from Nashville to Greenfield by himself, so he gave Johnny the gun in case "he had a flat tire or something."

When Buss held up the gun, Long identified it as the one he had given to Johnny, adding that he had gotten it as a Christmas gift from his mother.

Rick Long, John Long's brother, also testified in Johnny's defense. He was described as Johnny's security officer.

Rick Long testified that fans often got intoxicated and overzealous. He made the strange observation that those fans may pat Johnny on the back. Doing so, he explained, could cause Johnny, who had "emphysema and other lung problems," to lose his breath and cause the show to stop.

Rick Long went on to say that "Paycheck rarely goes out alone." Adding, "He's a real popular figure, and everywhere he goes, people recognize him and try to get close."

Larry "Red Dog" Adams testified that he was with Johnny earlier in the day on December 19. He confirmed that he was aware Johnny had a gun. Red Dog stated that Johnny dropped him off at his house before heading to the North High Lounge. After that, Red Dog went to bed and did not see Johnny again until around 5:00 the next morning, when he was getting ready for work. At that time, he found Johnny asleep on his couch.

Red Dog testified that when he arrived at work, a co-worker informed him that an all-points bulletin had been issued for Johnny's arrest. Upon hearing this, Red Dog decided to return home. For an unknown reason, he moved Johnny's car before going inside. There is no record of where he moved it to, but I presume he moved it farther away from his house; however, that is only a guess.

The police, assuming that Johnny may have fled to Red Dog's house, arrived shortly thereafter and arrested Johnny without incident.

Johnny Paycheck testified in his own defense. His attorney, Ralph Buss, tried to convince the jury that Wise and Bowers were bullying Johnny, causing him to feel intimidated and in danger before the shooting.

Johnny testified that after arriving at the North High Lounge, Lloyd Bowers approached him and said, "You son of a bitch, you're a pretty good singer."

To which Johnny replied, "Mister, you don't compliment me and insult me in the same breath."

Johnny also testified that Bowers said to him, "How in the hell did you get the name Paycheck when your name is Lytle?" Johnny said that comment really irritated him.

Continuing with his testimony, Johnny said that he asked Bowers and Wise to leave him alone and told them he would mess them up if they didn't. He also said that Bowers snatched his (Johnny's) hat off his (Johnny's) head, so Johnny snatched Bowers' hat off his (Bowers') head in retaliation, indicating that he did not trade hats willingly.

Johnny went on to say that Bowers told him, "There's 400 pounds of meat between us," meaning that Wise and Bowers had a combined weight of 400 pounds, and that was too much for Johnny to handle.

Johnny responded, "I don't care. You're messing with the wrong man."

After Judge Hottle overruled an objection from Prosecutor Coss, Johnny and his Attorney, Buss, demonstrated how the shooting occurred, using the gun as a prop. Coss referred to the demonstration as a "performance."

According to Johnny, Wise reached back and got a beer bottle and drank out of it while coming toward him.

Johnny said that he backed away and bumped against the jukebox, and that's when he reached for his gun. When he raised it, his finger slipped off the hammer, causing the gun to go off, with the bullet striking Wise.

"I was going to scare my way out... He went down, got right back up, and ran. I said, 'Wait a minute, man. I didn't mean to do that. And I didn't.'"

Johnny left the bar at that point and drove to Red Dog's house in Sabina. He testified that along the way, he threw the handgun out of the window, but he wasn't sure where.

Buss then raised the issue of New Year's when Johnny was at the Sunnyside Inn in Allensburg. The day before, Joyce Throckmorton, who had been at the bar that night, testified that Johnny told the crowd he shot Wise because "he needed it."

Johnny acknowledged making that statement but insisted it was just a joke. "It was just a little humor, just a little humor. I didn't need any more trouble," he explained.

On cross-examination, Johnny and Coss had a rather contentious exchange:

Coss: "You're a performer, right?"

Johnny: "Yes."

Coss: "You put on a show for people, right?"

Johnny: "Yes."

Coss: "You put on a show here, didn't you?"

Johnny, "No, I told the truth."

Coss: "How was it that you bought Bowers and Wise a drink and even traded hats with them, then ended up shooting one of the men?"

Johnny: "I bought the bar a beer. Not them specifically. I didn't trade hats. He took mine, and I took his. He jerked mine off me, and I jerked his off him. So we traded in a fashion."

Coss: "What happened to the beer bottle that Wise supposedly had in his hand and which you felt so threatened by? Would it have fallen to the floor?"

Johnny: "I guess so."

Coss: "The police officers that responded to the scene testified that there wasn't any broken glass on the barroom floor."

Johnny: "I can't answer that. Look, I never meant to shoot Larry. I just wanted to scare him off. If I'd been a shooting man, I would have shot him in the stomach."

Coss: "Were you drinking or indulging in cocaine during the day or night of December 18, the day before the shooting?"

Johnny: "No."

Coss: "If you were so nervous, why didn't you shoot Ernest Turner when he approached you after the shooting?"

Johnny: "I didn't shoot the other man on purpose. Why would I shoot Ernie?"

Coss: "Where has Bowers hat been since December 19?"

Johnny: "I'm not sure. Either with him or at the Adams' house. I don't sleep with it on. No."

Coss: "Have you ever seen this hat?" (Holding up Wise's Jack Daniel's hat with a bullet hole in it.)

Johnny: "No."

Coss: "How in the world did it get on the front seat of your car?"

Johnny: "I don't know."

Coss: "You planted this gun, didn't you, Mr. Paycheck? This isn't the gun you shot Mr. Wise with, is it?" (Holding up the gun.)

Johnny: "Yes, it is. I did not plant a gun anywhere."

Coss: "Does this gun appear to have laid outside for 17 or 18 days?"

Johnny: "I don't know. Did you clean it up?"

Coss: "Did you unload the bullets?"

Johnny: "No,"

Coss: "Shooting this man really bothered you… bothered you so much that you drove to Larry Adams', opened the refrigerator, turned on the TV, and fell asleep."

Johnny: "I hated that I did it."

The Hillsboro Press Gazette gave a more detailed account of the day's testimony in their May 15, 1986 edition.

City Editor Jeff Wooten quoted Wise as saying, "We were getting ready to leave, and Johnny was walking toward us. I guess he was leaving too, and Lloyd said, 'This is the guy who cooks turtle and deer meat.' Johnny then backed up, reached behind him, and the next thing I know, there's blood running down my face."

Lloyd Bowers' testimony about Johnny becoming angry at the mention of his brothers included Johnny saying he didn't like his brothers.

According to Johnny, Lloyd Bowers approached him at the bar, put a hand on his shoulder, and said, "You're Johnny Paycheck, aren't you? Do you remember me?" To which Johnny answered, "No."

Johnny further stated that Bowers approached him again, prompting Johnny to tell Bowers to leave him alone and threatening to mess him up.

At that point, according to Johnny, Dick McCormick asked Bowers to leave Johnny alone.

Johnny stated further, "The guy left. I was talking to Dick when he (Bowers) came back again. He jerked my hat off my head, and I jerked his hat off his head. He said 'trade?' And I said, 'Okay, let's trade.' Then he said, 'For a little son of a bitch, you sure can sing.'"

Attorney Buss asked Johnny if he told McCormick to shut up.

Johnny answered, "Yes, I did. These two guys were there, and I didn't want to take my eyes off them. That's why I told him to shut up and we'd leave in a minute.

Johnny said that he stood up when Bowers and Wise approached him again.

Bowers said, "Do you know this guy? This is Larry Wise."

That's when Johnny backed up against the jukebox.

In further testimony, Johnny said that Bowers asked him if he had a place to stay and said that they would feed him deer meat and turtle soup. "Like I was a bum, you know," Johnny added.

"I said 'what do you take me for, a country hick that blew into town yesterday?' I told them they were messing with the wrong guy."

On May 16, the jury of eight men and four women deliberated for nearly three hours before finding Johnny guilty of aggravated assault and tampering with evidence, but innocent of carrying a concealed weapon. He was sentenced to 7 to 9.5 years in prison.

According to Gary Adams, who attended every day of the trial, as Johnny was being led from the courtroom, he turned and said, "I'll be out in two weeks."

After sentencing, Judge Hottle, at the request of Highland County Sheriff Earl Mahaffey, ordered Johnny to be transported to the Brown County Jail in Mount Orab. Sheriff Mahaffey made this request because several individuals from Greenfield were being held in the Highland County Jail, and he believed it was best for Johnny not to be housed with them.

Sheriff Mahaffey was quoted in the May 20 edition of *The Hillsboro Press Gazette* as saying, "I'd rather have him write a song about the Brown County Jail than the Highland County Jail."

Johnny's attorney, Ralph Buss, promptly filed an appeal with the Ohio 4th District Court of Appeals. On May 26, after posting a $50,000 cash bond*** Johnny was released from jail while his appeal was pending.

Speaking with the press immediately after his release, Johnny spoke highly of the Brown County Jail, where he had been held since his conviction. "If you gotta be in jail, Brown County is probably the finest people to be with," he said. He also praised the media, saying, "The media has treated me good through the whole thing."

The following evening, on May 27, just eleven days after being convicted, Johnny was performing with George Jones at the Jones Country Amusement Park in Colmesneil, Texas. On May 28, he had an engagement in Arizona for a benefit concert supporting "Hands Across America."

Meanwhile, his latest single, "The Old Violin," sat at number 51 on the country music charts.

For the next 33 months, Johnny remained free, and he performed shows all across the country. During this time, he released two albums: *Modern Times* in March 1987, which reached number 54 on the charts, and a gospel album titled *Outlaw at the Cross* in November 1988, although that one did not chart. It is noteworthy that Johnny donated his royal-

---

1. *** *The $50,000 cash bond is believed to have been provided by George Jones and Merle Haggard, as well as Jerry Lee Lewis who contributed $1,400, according to Ralph Buss.*

ties from these albums to a Los Angeles-based charity that supports children with AIDS. Neither album produced any memorable singles.

After losing his appeal to the Ohio 4th District Court of Appeals on August 19, 1988, Johnny's defense requested that the Ohio Supreme Court postpone the resentencing hearing indefinitely while pursuing another appeal. However, the Supreme Court declined this request. As a result, Johnny's resentencing hearing took place on February 6, 1989, in the Highland County Common Pleas Court.

Attorney Ralph Buss hoped that Johnny's pleas would convince Judge Hottle to reduce or suspend his sentence.

While on the stand, Johnny told Judge Hottle that the only reason he was asking for mercy was "so I could work." Johnny said that he needed to make money by playing concerts because his family had no health insurance, and he was paying cash for his wife's medical bills. "It is for her and my family that I must keep working... If I'm taken away, my wife will be dead in six months."

When questioned about treatment for alcohol and substance abuse, Johnny said that he had been in and out of treatment for alcohol abuse but never for drugs. He also added that he hadn't consumed any alcohol since the trial.

Four character witnesses testified on Johnny's behalf, each providing glowing endorsements. Songwriter Kenneth McDuffey, who had known Johnny since 1963, described him as a "humanitarian." Jane Ann Adams, Johnny's longtime friend and the wife of Red Dog Adams, painted him as "a giving and loving person." Johnny's publisher and producer, Billy Don Burns, spoke to the court about Johnny's new gospel album, stating that all proceeds would go to charity. Additionally, his business manager and lead guitarist, John Ray Long, shared details about Johnny's hospitalizations for emphysema and asthma since the trial began.

Prosecutor Rocky Coss urged the judge to re-impose the original sentence of 7 to 9.5 years, stating, "The defendant has always taken the position that Johnny Paycheck should be treated differently." He emphasized that the defendant's history did not reflect that of a humanitarian. Coss pointed to Johnny's past convictions, which include stealing cars, malicious mischief, and passing bad checks. He also mentioned Johnny's no-contest plea related to a case in Wyoming involving inappropriate conduct with a 12-year-old girl.

"Perhaps he has changed his life around since the conviction, but that's to be expected," Coss continued, saying that everything that Johnny had done since 1986 was obviously geared toward gaining sympathy from the court and pointing out that Johnny's wife was diagnosed with cancer five years ago, before the North High Lounge incident. "Five years ago was the time to change," he added.

After considering the testimony, Judge Hottle, while sharing about his own battle with cancer, and expressing sympathy for Johnny, imposed the same sentence as at trial: 7 to 9.5 years.

Johnny was handcuffed and taken to the Highland County Jail. By mid-February, he was transferred to the Orient Correctional Reception Center, south of Columbus for processing into the Ohio prison system.

In an interview published in the February 27 *Columbus Dispatch*, Johnny said that he would continue writing songs while in prison, but didn't think he would ever write a song about the shooting.

In another interview published the same day in the *Newark Advocate*, Johnny said, "We didn't have no insurance. When I had the money, and I could have put it away, I didn't have much sense." Referring to his plea for mercy at his sentencing hearing.

After completing processing, Johnny was transferred to the Chillicothe Correctional Institution, located just 30 minutes from Greenfield, to serve his sentence.

Four months later, on June 13, Merle Haggard visited the prison, and he performed a concert for the inmates alongside Johnny. The show was recorded with plans to release it as a documentary film and an album. However, as of the writing of this book, neither the film nor the album has been released.

On January 10, 1991, Ohio Governor Richard Celeste commuted Johnny's sentence, allowing him to be released from prison after serving twenty-two months. Celeste issued Johnny's commutation along with eight others for death row inmates during the final days of his term. A petition signed by fans, friends, and fellow entertainers had been presented to the governor several weeks earlier, requesting a pardon. It is possible that Larry Wise also signed the petition and wrote letters on Johnny's behalf, but I have not confirmed this information.

Prosecutor Rocky Coss opposed Johnny's release, arguing it was due solely to his celebrity status.

While commuting Johnny's sentence, Governor Celeste ordered that Johnny complete 200 hours of community service and remain alcohol-free.

Johnny completed his community service by speaking to youth groups nationwide about the dangers of drugs and alcohol. All reports confirm that Johnny remained alcohol-free for the rest of his life.

After Johnny was released from prison, he stopped wearing his big black hat. He had fully abandoned the outlaw persona.

Chapter 43

New Information

During my research for this book, I came across new information.

First of all, while most accounts do suggest that Johnny visited Paul Angel in Greenfield, I learned a different angle regarding that visit during my interview with Don Adams on June 14, 2025. According to Don, on the day of the shooting, Johnny arrived at Paul's house in Greenfield, where Angel and the Adams boys, Don, Gary, and Arnie, were gathered in the basement, talking and playing music. Don recalled, "He (Johnny) was stoned out of his mind when he came in. He didn't hang around long. There was a pistol tucked in his waistband, and he was really jittery, pacing around the basement. He looked like hell. He went to leave, and when he got to the door, he turned around and said, 'I'm gonna shoot some sumbitch tonight.'"

I don't know if Johnny was making a promise or just having a premonition.

On January 8, 2026, I reached out to Lloyd Bowers' daughter, Mary Jo, who had been a childhood classmate of mine. I asked her to convince her father to agree to an interview. After some persuasion, Bowers finally agreed to speak with me. On January 11, we had a brief phone conversation. Then, on January 19, I made the three-hour trip from my home in Danville, KY, to Greenfield to meet him.

On my way to Greenfield, I recorded a 30-second Facebook video to announce my intention to interview Bowers. Within 48 hours, it received over 1 million views, and by the time this book was released, it had over 2 million views.

Upon arriving in Greenfield, I called Bowers, but he had a change of heart and said he wasn't sure he would have time for the interview after all. However, the next day, January 20, he indicated that he would be willing to chat with me over the phone. I called him, and we had a conversation that lasted about 35 minutes.

I was genuinely shocked when Bowers confirmed that he had never been interviewed about the shooting before. This struck me as very odd, considering he was not only an eyewitness to a high-profile crime involving a well-known celebrity, but he was also directly involved in the events that led up to the shooting.

I asked Bowers to explain what happened that night at the North High Lounge. He told me that he and Larry Wise were sitting in a booth at the back of the bar, talking to a man named Jimmy Kniesly, who was from Greenfield. Kniesly had a band that was performing at the bar that night. During their conversation, Kniesly mentioned that Johnny was at the bar, prompting Bowers to go over and talk to him.

Bowers said that he sat down at the bar next to Paycheck and introduced himself. The two started talking, and Bowers told Johnny that he knew his brothers, Jack, Pete, and Bob Lytle. According to Bowers, Johnny's demeanor changed when his brothers were mentioned.

According to Bowers, Johnny said, "I don't want to talk about my family. My family is out."

So Bowers, trying to change the subject, removed his hat, laid it on the bar, and said, "How about we trade?"

Johnny said, "Okay," and they swapped hats, each putting the other's hat on their head.

About that time, Wise came to the bar and introduced himself to Johnny. Wise told Johnny that some guys were going to his house to play music and invited him to join them, adding that he would cook up some turtle meat. For some reason, Johnny was insulted by that comment, so he drew his pistol, pointed it at Wise, and shot.

I asked Bowers if Wise raised a beer bottle at Johnny as if he was going to hit him.

"No," said Bowers. "At least not that I saw. And I was standing right there. Larry hit the floor, then he jumped up and ran out. Then Paycheck ran out, and it seemed like the cops were right there about the same time."

"I thought it must not hit him or something," Bowers continued, "because Larry just jumped up and ran out. I said there's got to be blood, so I went out to look for Larry. There was blood, so I tracked him up the street to the Merchants Bank. He was squatted down (in the doorway) and had his hand on his head. There was blood, but not much."

When asked if Paycheck appeared drunk or high, Bowers answered, "Yeah, he looked like he was on something."

I asked Bowers what Johnny said before he ran out.

"He might have said, 'I'm out of here,' but I'm not sure," Bowers answered.

Bowers mentioned that he didn't see Johnny outside because Johnny's car was parked at the opposite end of the street, suggesting he was probably already gone.

I brought up the accusations Johnny's attorney made against him and Wise, alleging bullying. "Was there anything that could have been taken as bullying or messing with Paycheck?" I asked.

"That was all bullshit," Bowers answered. "You know how lawyers are. They never tell the whole story. Lawyers are just a bunch of crooks. Judges too. We weren't looking for no trouble. He got mad when I said I know'd his brothers and he shot Larry when he invited him (Johnny) to his house."

Without prompting, Bowers told me that a day or two after the shooting, Arnie and Don Adams paid a visit to Wise and asked him not to file charges against Johnny.

In an earlier interview for this book, Don stated that, before the trial, Gary, representing an unidentified group, approached Larry Wise with an offer of $50,000. The proposal was for Wise to testify that the gun belonged to him, that the shooting was accidental, and to request that the charges be dropped. Don said that Wise declined the offer.

It is unclear how much, if any, pressure the Adams brothers exerted on Larry Wise. They may have simply asked him nicely, or perhaps they were more insistent. It's difficult to say. Regardless, Larry Wise ultimately filed a civil suit against Johnny. Unfortunately, I have not been able to find any information regarding the outcome of that lawsuit.

I asked Bowers about Wise's feelings towards Johnny after the shooting.

"He never really said much about it. People joked around with us about it all the time, but it kind of wasn't a big deal most of the time," Bowers said.

"Did Larry hate Paycheck after that?" I asked.

"I don't really think he hated him or nothing like that. He never said that anyway," Bowers replied.

The last thing I discussed with Bowers was Mike Judge's animated show, *Tales from the Tour Bus*. I asked him if anyone had reached out to him during the show's production, especially since he and Larry Wise are prominently featured in the first episode. He responded that no one ever contacted him. I then inquired about his thoughts on how he and Wise were portrayed, as well as the show's accuracy in depicting the shooting. He mentioned that he couldn't comment on it because he had never watched the show, aside from a short clip he had seen on YouTube.

In addition to the Lloyd Bowers interview, four people reached out to me on their own accord with information about the shooting incident.

On December 18, 2025, a man, I'll call him Todd, who claimed to have been incarcerated with Johnny at the Orient Correctional Reception Center, sent me a message on Facebook. He said that Johnny referred to himself as "Donald Eugene" while he was locked up there, and that "He acted just like everyone else."

On January 20, 2026, a man from Greenfield, we'll call him Chuck, sent me a copy of a one page letter that Johnny allegedly wrote to Wise apologizing for shooting him. Chuck got the copy from a relative of Larry Wise who allegedly has possession of the original. The undated letter is written on prison letterhead from the Chillicothe Correctional Institute

(CCI), and the signature matches samples of Johnny's signature that I have seen. It appears to be legitimate.

In the letter, Johnny begins by saying, "*Dear Larry, it's been almost three yrs. since the incident occurred between us.*" However, since Johnny didn't arrive at CCI until mid to late February 1989 and the shooting happened on December 19, 1985, it had actually been just over three years.

The letter goes on to say, "*... I feel in my heart that I owe you an apology.*"

It is signed:

"*Sincerely,*

I hope your friend –

Johnny Paycheck"

It's worth noting that the letter is well written. It is legible, free of spelling errors, and contains proper punctuation.

On February 23, 2026, a woman I have known for years, told me she worked at the Orient Correctional Reception Center when Johnny arrived there shortly after his sentencing. Carla's job was to interview prisoners regarding past drug and alcohol use. Johnny told her that he NEVER used drugs and only occasionally consumed alcohol. I will let that claim rest on its own merit.

On February 18, 2026, I received a message from Greg Smith, a musician from Sabina, OH, who knew the Adams Boys and Johnny Paycheck quite well and was good friends with Gary Adams and Larry "Red Dog" Adams. He also played music with Ralph May in California for several years as part of Ralph's Ohio River Band.

Smith told me that he was present at Red Dog's house when police arrested Johnny on the morning of December 20, 1985, and he agreed to be interviewed for the book.

According to Smith, he was home from California for Christmas and staying with his parents in Sabina. Having just arrived home a few hours earlier. Smith was asleep when he received a call from Jane Ann Adams in the wee hours of the morning on December 20. Jane Ann told him about the shooting and that Johnny was at her and Red Dog's house. The police were outside their home by then, and Jane Ann wanted Smith to come over and take their daughter, Lori Adams, out of the house so she would not be present when Johnny was arrested. The thought being that it would be too emotionally charged for her since Johnny was a good friend of the family.

So Smith got dressed and drove to Red Dog's house, which was just a few minutes away, to do as Jane Ann had asked. Upon arrival, Smith noticed a large police presence in the neighborhood. He was allowed to enter the home, and he saw Johnny sitting at the kitchen table.

"Johnny was looking pretty worried," Smith said. "You could tell that he knew he had messed up, and it was very serious."

I asked him what the Adams family's demeanor was at the time. He said that Jane Ann and Lori were visibly upset to the point of crying, and that Red Dog had a worried look on his face and kept looking out the window.

Smith left with Lori Adams and drove a few miles to a truck stop, where they stayed for about an hour before driving back to Red Dog's house.

"We stayed at the truck stop for quite a while. At least an hour, I'd say, then we drove back to Red Dog's. I assumed that they had taken Paycheck away by then. But that wasn't the case," Smith said.

Arriving back at Red Dog's house, Smith and Lori Adams walked in the front door, and Johnny was standing in the living room, handcuffed, next to a Clinton County sheriff's deputy. I asked Smith how many police officers were in the house. He said he only remembered seeing the one, but acknowledged there were probably more.

Smith said Lori Adams became very emotional at that point and was crying with Jane Ann.

"You could tell that Johnny was really upset at seeing the women cry. He told them that everything would be okay and asked them not to cry. He was trying to comfort them," said Smith.

Finally, Johnny was led out of the house, placed in the back of a police cruiser, and transported back to Hillsboro.

Chapter 44

My Verdict

I have studied this case extensively. I've reviewed sworn testimonies, read media reports, interviewed eyewitnesses, and listened to the opinions and arguments of both Johnny Paycheck fans and critics for the past four decades.

Despite that, several aspects of the case leave me with questions.

I was born and raised in Greenfield, OH, and I've heard the story of the North High Lounge incident countless times since 1985. However, I don't remember hearing about the Peruvian cocaine and the suitcases filled with cash until the late 2010s. Around the same time that the show *Tales from the Tour Bus* aired.

No one ever insinuated during his trial that Johnny drove to Greenfield from Maryland while transporting large amounts of cocaine and cash. In fact, there is ample evidence to indicate that Johnny did, in fact, drive to Greenfield from

Nashville. At no point did the Prosecution ever challenge that.

If Johnny really did drive from Maryland to Greenfield, what happened to the stash of Peruvian cocaine and the two suitcases full of cash that he brought with him? Did Johnny hide them, planning to retrieve them later? Did he give them to someone for safekeeping? Were they discovered during his arrest but simply "overlooked"? Are they still out there somewhere, waiting to be found? Or could that part of the story be a fabrication?

My gut tells me that IF the Maryland incident truly occurred, it was a separate event that happened before the Hillsboro incident; over time, the two might have merged. That's how legends often develop.

The same applies to Don's claim that Johnny brandished a gun at Paul Angel's house and promised to "Shoot some sumbitch tonight." Did that really happen? Don said it did, so I will take him at his word. However, like the claim from Maryland, this incident never came up in court.

I suspect there was an occasion where Johnny brandished a gun at Paul Angel's house, mentioning something about shooting someone. Did this occur on the night of the shooting in Hillsboro? I don't believe it did. Instead, I think it occurred before December 18, 1985. Don simply made an honest mistake in connecting that incident to the shooting.

I often reference Mike Judge's show, *Tales from the Tour Bus*. It's an excellent series, and I'm a big fan, particularly of the first two episodes that prominently feature the Adams Boys alongside Johnny Paycheck and George Jones. If you haven't watched it yet, I recommend doing so after you've read this book. That said, the show has likely had a significantly oversized influence on what many people know, or think they know, about the shooting. Like most accounts, perhaps even the one you're reading, it contains both accurate and inaccurate details.

There are a few points made in the show that are revealing. Defense attorney Ralph Buss discusses his decision to have Johnny testify in his own defense. Almost immediately, Buss expresses regret about this choice, describing Johnny as appearing disheveled and looking "dangerous and close to psychotic," adding that "he was so high." Buss even goes so far as to say that Johnny resembled Charles Manson.

Prosecutor Rocky Coss recalled that, in full view of the jury, Johnny picked up the gun used in the crime and spun it around on his finger, much like a gunfighter in an old Western movie. This action may have ultimately sealed Johnny's fate.

Another discrepancy involves Johnny's condition the night of the shooting. Don Adams described him as being "stoned out of his mind" when he allegedly came to Paul Angel's house hours before the shooting.

On episode 1 of *Tales From The Tour Bus*, Johnny is presented as being "extremely high on cocaine."

Only one witness from the shooting testified that Johnny appeared to be high. During the trial, North High Lounge owner Ernest Turner stated that Johnny did not seem intoxicated.

In his closing argument, Prosecutor Rocky Coss made only a brief reference to drugs and alcohol.

Most importantly, the media did not widely report that Johnny was under the influence of drugs or alcohol. Wouldn't the media be quick to cover any suggestion that Johnny was intoxicated? The answer is, "YES."

Was Johnny drinking that night? Of course, he was. He was in a bar. That's what people do in bars. Was he a little tipsy? Probably. Was he extremely high on cocaine? Probably not.

Why is there a discrepancy? I believe the story sounds better if Johnny is high on cocaine. It seems plausible that Johnny was under the influence that night; however, the trial record does not support this.

I offer my conclusive opinion on what is true, what are lies, what is myth, and what is legend.

Did Johnny Paycheck arrive in Greenfield on December 19, 1985, with a car full of Peruvian cocaine and two suitcases of cash? Absolutely not.

Did Johnny Paycheck announce his intention to shoot someone in Paul Angel's basement before driving to Hillsboro and gunning down Larry Wise? Absolutely not.

Did the offer of a late-night supper, consisting of a savory turtle soup, enrage Johnny Paycheck so much that he drew a gun and shot chef Larry Wise? Absolutely not.

Then why did Johnny Paycheck shoot Larry Wise? According to Lloyd Bowers, the story about turtle soup was made up by a newspaper reporter. While he confirmed that they did discuss cooking some turtle meat, Bowers stated that neither he nor Larry Wise ever mentioned turtle soup, and any claims to the contrary are untrue. He said he had never even heard of turtle soup before. Bowers explained that, in his opinion, the only way to eat turtle meat was fried. He also reiterated that referencing Johnny's brothers is what initially irritated him, and things went downhill from there.

Johnny Paycheck was driven to shoot Larry Wise for two simple reasons: he was intoxicated, and he feared for his safety.

Johnny's defense never argued that Johnny didn't shoot Larry Wise. Instead, Ralph Buss sought to persuade the jury that Johnny acted in self-defense. He argued that Lloyd Bowers and Larry Wise were bullying Johnny.

Two men that Johnny did not know approached him in a bar. These men were bigger and younger than the

5-foot-5-inch, 47-year-old country music star. All three of them had been drinking, and their manner of speaking r-eflected typical barroom conversation: loud, unfiltered, and somewhat aggressive; almost performative. I know this be-cause I've done it myself while hanging out in bars in my younger days. And I've seen others do it as well.

Johnny was not only physically small, but he was also in the early stages of emphysema and asthma, which made him feel unhealthy. Additionally, he was considered by many to be a nervous person. He was always aware of his surroundings and remained on guard, feeling vulnerable as a result.

I don't doubt that Johnny felt bullied. He was aware of his physical limitations, had been drinking alcohol, and was nat-urally nervous. However, Bowers and Wise were not actually bullying him. They had been drinking as well and were caught up in the typical behavior of intoxicated individuals, which includes obnoxious actions and speech. They were simply a couple of drunk guys having a conversation with another drunk guy. It wasn't bullying; they may have been teasing Johnny, playfully pushing his buttons, so to speak. This is what guys consider locker room talk, which tends to be rough, especially when women and children aren't present.

Johnny interpreted their actions as a threat. His response was to pull his gun, cock the hammer, level it at Larry Wise, and squeeze the trigger.

It's important to note that the gun Johnny was carrying was a single-action revolver, meaning it could only be fired after cocking the hammer and then squeezing the trigger. A sober Johnny Paycheck might have drawn the gun, but likely wouldn't have fired it. An intoxicated Johnny Paycheck though, did fire the gun albeit, I believe, unintentionally. The moral of the story? Alcohol and guns don't mix.

On the other hand, I don't buy the "We didn't do anything" defense that the Prosecution presented through the testimony of Bowers and Wise. As mentioned earlier, they were likely giving Johnny a hard time. Everyone in the bar reported witnessing two separate arguments, and Johnny wasn't arguing with himself. However, they didn't do anything that warranted being shot.

What about the gun presented at the trial as the one used in the crime?

It was found in a creek bed after lying there for "17 or 18 days." When Jim Wilson discovered it, the gun was rust-free and had no live or empty cartridges in the cylinder. A quick search of the weather in southwest Ohio during December 1985 revealed colder-than-normal temperatures. On December 17, one day before the shooting, most of the area received 1.5 inches of snow on top of 0.5 inches already on the ground. Temperatures began to rise on New Year's Day, reaching the mid-40s by January 2. On January 5, eighteen days after the shooting, another half inch of snow fell. The environment would have been very wet by the time the gun was found, and the gun would surely be covered in rust. I seriously doubt that this was the weapon used in the shooting.

For the record, no ballistic tests were conducted to link the gun to the crime. Why? Because the fragments from the bullet that struck Wise were too small to be tested, and no empty casing was recovered since the gun was not loaded when it was found.

Where did the gun presented at the trial come from? If I had to guess, I would say that Johnny Paycheck or an associate of his planted it in the frozen creek and led Jim Wilson to it. Was Wilson involved in the deception? My guess is no. I suspect that the actual gun is still lying in a field somewhere in Highland or Clinton Counties.

Then there are the stories about the Adams boys and their contact with Larry Wise after the shooting. Are those stories true? I believe they are. Remember, Johnny was their lifelong friend, so who could blame them for trying to help him?

Lloyd Bowers saw Arnie and Don at Larry Wise's house in the days following the shooting. According to him, they asked Wise not to pursue a case against Johnny. Additionally, Don told me that Gary approached Wise with an offer of $50,000 to testify that it was all an accident and that it was actually his gun that was used.

It's important to note that Don, Gary, and Arnie, known, with good reason, as the Notorious Adams Boys, were well-versed in navigating such situations.

My verdict: Johnny Paycheck argued with Larry Wise and Lloyd Bowers. All three were somewhat intoxicated. Johnny felt threatened. Johnny pulled a gun and shot Wise. Johnny didn't intend to shoot, only to frighten; he intentionally cocked the hammer and unintentionally squeezed the trigger. Johnny was negligent in shooting Wise, but dammit, he didn't intend to do it. That said, he was guilty.

Think about everything you've heard and read about this incident since 1985, and decide for yourself how you want to contribute to its legacy moving forward. I've made my own decision, and if I don't do anything else, I will argue with anyone that claims Johnny Paycheck shot Larry Wise over turtle soup.

Final Note from the Author

Well, folks, that's it.

I started this book fifteen months ago. I finished it fifteen minutes ago.

In between, I drank too damn much coffee, dealt with life's bullshit, fought through stretches where I couldn't write a sentence, and spent more dark mornings than I can count staring at a screen wondering if anyone would care.

Don Adams died before I could finish. That hurt.

But I kept my promise. I told their story. Every wild night, every knock-out punch, every moment the world should've remembered but didn't.

Writing this book damn near killed me. I'm proud of it. I'm exhausted. And I'm grateful you're holding it.

The Adams Boys deserved this.
Now you know why.
—Eric Grate
Danville, KY
April 28, 2026

Eric Grate "King of the Legendary Saturday Nights" Downtown Greenfield on the Johnny Paycheck Bench January 19, 2026 Photo by Eric Grate

About the Author

Eric Grate is a writer, Marine Corps veteran, photographer, and coffeehouse owner from Danville, Kentucky. Born and raised in Greenfield, Ohio, Grate brings a small-town authenticity to his work, rooted in small-town life, humor, and Americana realism.

He began writing in his mid-fifties and has since published The Streets of Greenfield (2023) and Snapshots in Time (2024), two acclaimed short story collections rooted in Americana realism.

The Notorious Adams Boys marks his first nonfiction release.

Contact: Eric Grate
Email: eric@ericgrate.com
Website: www.ericgrate.com
Facebook: @EricGrateAuthor